Fifty *and* Other F-Words

FLABBY
FEARLESS
FRAZZLED
FORLORN
FLUMMOXED
FLEXIBLE
FLAMBOYANT
FASHIONABLE
FEMINIST
FREE

Fifty and Other F-Words

REFLECTIONS FROM THE REARVIEW MIRROR

Margot Potter

STERLING

New York

STERLING
New York

An Imprint of Sterling Publishing Co., Inc.
1166 Avenue of the Americas
New York, NY 10036

ISBN 978-1-4549-2796-9

Library of Congress Cataloging-in-Publication Data

Names: Potter, Margot, author.
Title: Fifty and other F-words : reflections from the rearview mirror /
   Margot Potter.
Description: New York, NY : Sterling Publishing Co., Inc., [2018] |
Includes
   bibliographical references and index.
Identifiers: LCCN 2018000117 (print) | LCCN 2018004938 (ebook) | ISBN
   9781454927976 (e-book) | ISBN 9781454927969 (hardcover : alk. paper)
Subjects: LCSH: Middle age--Humor. | Middle-aged women--Humor.
Classification: LCC PN6231.M47 (ebook) | LCC PN6231.M47 P68 2018 (print) |
   DDC 818/.602--dc23
LC record available at
https://lccn.loc.gov/2018000117

CONTENTS

DEDICATION

One day, my dear Avalon, you will turn 50. If all goes as planned, I'll be there to offer you a snifter of wine and a sprinkling of confetti. If I cannot be there due to unforeseen circumstances, I wrote this book. It may provide some small comfort or moment of comic relief. I make no promises, except these two. I love you. You're going to be just fine. Mr. Potter, I don't have a medal to bestow upon you for surviving the dual onslaught of menopause and puberty, but here's a loving mention in the dedication of this book. Mom, I have no idea how you did any of it and did it all with such grace, but I do know that I'm in awe of your magnificence and deeply indebted to you for showing me how to be a kick-ass warrior woman of the highest order.

This is a book about life after 50. It will make you laugh, it will make you think, it will make you cry, it might even make you hungry. You're probably already experiencing all of these things simultaneously. Am I right? This is the story of how I've met the challenges of navigating my 50s, and incorporates the lessons I've drawn from staring down the fifth decade of my life. It's a look at the good, the bad, the ugly, the wrinkled, the sagging, and the hairy. I'm letting it all hang out and down past my knees without apology. It may not be pretty, but it's honest. In sharing my truth, I'm hoping to inspire you to find yours.

When we enter our midlife years, we have an opportunity. We may be facing the empty nest, mourning changes in our appearance, transitioning into a new career, or finding our interpersonal relationships evolving. We are losing some things, but between those losses a space is opening for something new. We can opt to fill the empty space with doodads from discount department stores or set forth on glorious new adventures. We can feel sorry about what we've lost, or celebrate what we've gained. We can cherish the past while looking forward to a deeper, richer, more complex relationship with our grown children, significant others, the world at large, and, most importantly, with ourselves. The last call for baby making may be past, but it's time to hit the after party! Glitter up those eyelids and rave on, Mama!

There is life after 50, real life, soulful, magical, kick-ass, beautiful life. We aren't relegated to the sidelines and we do not have to fade away. In fact, this is the perfect time to dial up the volume. At this age, we've earned the right to do whatever makes us happy and be who we are without shame, fear, or apology. The truth is, we always had that right. We live in a youth-obsessed culture, but we don't have to accept that meme. We are strong, powerful women with the power to change the discourse. It starts with us, refusing to become invisible. It means daring to live out loud, coloring outside of the lines, and rewriting the current scripts on aging.

Age is just a number and attitude is everything. Toss out that old road map: You're forging your own path. Hell yes, you're 50, and you're just getting started, darling.

Cheers,
Margot

ONE *fearless*

YOU'RE HERE.
YOU'RE 50.
GET OVER IT.

Somehow, and utterly without explanation, I reached my midcentury mark in much the same sour pickle as I had 10 years earlier. My fading career was a grand invention born of an intoxicating mix of desperation, fortitude, and hope. At 39, I was a woman clinging to a tenuous lifeline, resolutely making it up every day on my computer, on a tiny table between the stove and the refrigerator. Everything in my life had fallen apart professionally. I felt utterly bereft and adrift. I spent my 39th year wavering between flailing about aimlessly and purposefully swimming toward a new shore. I was being buoyed by belief in my worth, my talent, my creativity, and my ability to magically transform my life from ruin into joy. Defying all logic, I did it. In the process of my grand reinvention, I raised an exceptional young woman with a wonderful, kind, supportive husband. Yup, I did that, and looking back on what I've accomplished over the past 13 years, I'm mightily chuffed. Even if it hasn't always been a bed of glitter, it's been a wonderful, wild ride. It is not over yet, not by a long shot.

I struggled with my 50th birthday, in much the same way that I struggled with my 40th. I asked myself why I wasn't "there yet," as if there was a there and there was a way of knowing that you'd arrived. "Am I there yet? Am I almost there? How will I know? Is there a road sign to alert me? How do I get there and how long can I stay there before they kick me out?"

I made room on my shelves for adult diapers and a prescription for osteoporosis medicine. I stocked up on comfort shoes and compression hose. I grudgingly signed up for the AARP and got my discount card. With menopause under way, I prepared to save a fortune on feminine products and permanently avoid toxic shock syndrome. Not to mention reveling in the sheer joy of waving a permanent farewell to Auntie Flo.

I never liked that bitch anyway.

I'd arrived at the big five-o. 50. As I pulled into the turnstile, I was met with a plethora of vexing changes. Weight gain, check. Jowl formation, check. Neck collapse, in progress. Sagging parts, here! Old lady hands, hello. Side boobs, egads! Suddenly nothing fits quite the way it did before. I have developed what I'm calling old lady arms. That saggy, fatty flesh that droops sadly over your elbows—what the hell is that?

I did not order that. Send it back!

The thing is, I don't see any of it until I look at a photograph of myself. In my mind and in my mirror, I still look fabulous. And perhaps that solitary delusion of grandeur will be my saving grace.

Is it just me, or is it weird to think that at 50 all of the rules change without any fanfare? Who makes these decisions? And why?

I have a secret for you: 50 doesn't feel much different from 49. It doesn't feel much different from 39, either, at least not mentally. There isn't a tectonic shift. That's the strange thing about aging—it happens incrementally. You don't see the subtle changes until you see a photo or a video or a reflection as you pass by the mirror under unflattering light and realize that you aren't the you that you are used to being. Then you have to decide how you feel about that, because you can't turn back time. You don't feel older until you try to do something you've always done and find it suddenly more difficult. Time progresses, gravity pulls, collagen departs, estrogen exits stage left, and you get older. If you're lucky.

There are many schools of thought on aging. The prevailing one is that women should "age gracefully." I'm not exactly sure what that means. Aging gracefully is vaguely defined as dressing conservatively, getting a sensible haircut, wearing less makeup, acting your age, speaking softly, and fading into the background, all of which sounds hideous to me. This is all in the service of making older women less noticeable. Women are supposed to start becoming invisible when they turn 50 to make room for the newer models. We're terrified of aging in this culture, thanks to the unrelenting stream of media messaging that older women are unattractive, boring, and disposable. We worship youth and beauty with a frenetic obsession. Women in their 20s are getting Botox®. Fashion models start work in their teens and age out long before 30. Actresses over 40 are counting the days until their last leading role. Women over 50 are finding it increasingly difficult to get and maintain a job.

When I look at the "What to Wear at Any Age" spreads in the fashion magazines, I have magically moved into the 50s category. Just like that. Apparently, until I turn the corner into my 70s, I'm supposed to steer clear of outfits that remotely resemble anything fun. According to the fashion police, most of whom are in their 20s, women should not wear miniskirts after 40. Women of a certain age should not wear leggings, and no women should wear leggings as pants. Women over 50 should not wear their hair past their shoulders, and it should definitely not be dyed outrageous colors. Women over 50 should not curse in public. Women over 50 should refrain from dancing on tabletops.

I'm not a fan of rules. I haven't been keen on obeying them up to this point. It seems silly to start now.

> **ONE OF THE** bonuses of turning 50 is that you care far less about what other people think. You get to decide every day how to dress, what to do, and what to say. The truth is, you always did.

Five years into my 50s and you'd think by this point I'd have it down. I don't. I'm not sure one ever gets this stuff down. I have a sneaking suspicion that as soon as we master a decade, we've already slid into the next one. That's been my experience so far. I look back with hard-earned wisdom. I want to tell my younger self all of this cool stuff that I've learned. The words would mean little without the added benefit of experience. Younger folks are prone to ignoring the heartfelt advice of older people. Even if I could travel back in time to meet the younger me without disrupting the fabric of space and time, I'm not sure my efforts would be fruitful.

BECOMING INVISIBLE

Women who are past the age of procreation and raising children are, for biological purposes, irrelevant. Men can keep making babies until they die, but that window closes for women after menopause. It bears pondering: Is biological irrelevance our enemy? That loss of hormones also signals the end of our youth. We've been enculturated to fear older women. My gorgeous mother, who is now in her 70s, has been telling me for years that she feels as if she's disappeared. People literally don't see her. Even celebrated beauties will bemoan the double standard they face.

Sure, disappearing after 50 might be a negative, but ponder the possibilities! Invisibility does sound intriguing. Instead of fighting the inevitable, why not embrace it? Think of the fun you can have once you're completely transparent! You'll be free to walk around buck naked on hot days. Hallelujah! The emperor has no clothes, and neither will you. Diets? Nothing's skinnier than invisible. Bring on the bacon, wrap it in a flaky pastry, and top it with butter, baby. You can stop worrying if men find you pretty and focus on more important things, like cultivating your brain or taking up topless gardening. Let your wrinkles proliferate and set those gray hairs free. You'll save a fortune on anti-aging creams and hair products. Best of all, you can finally become the woman you've always been without apology, explanation, or the need to hide behind the illusion of giving a rat's ass what other people think.

IN SEARCH OF THAT GIRL

Once upon a time I was a single gal. I was wild, unfettered, and free. I was saucy. I was naughty. I was sexy. I was outrageous. I changed my hair color the way most people change socks. I wore blood-red lipstick and kohl-black eyeliner. I said whatever I wanted to say and did whatever I pleased whenever it pleased me. I had an ass off which one could bounce a quarter and a totally rockin' bod. I could wear absolutely anything and look fabulous in it, like a super model or a 19-year-old. I could stay out all night or stay in all night and I didn't have to answer to a single, solitary soul. I kissed the boys and made them cry. I danced on tabletops and on stages and down sidewalks in the middle of the day. I was the master of my own destiny. I was a pirate and the world was my ocean. I sailed my ship through stormy seas and through fair weather and to distant and exotic shores. I took what I wanted without shame. I had incredible adventures. Oh, yes, I did.

I was lonely, yes. I had my heart broken often. I had a knack for falling in love with the wrong kind of men. It was hard to come home at the end of a long day and have no one with whom to share my stories, but it was lovely to come home at the end of a long day and draw a warm bubble bath, crank up the stereo, and relax without distractions. It was also lovely to sleep in until noon, if I so chose. The only person I had to worry about was me. My house was impeccably clean; my pillows didn't have holes chewed in them or juice boxes spilled on them or mysterious gray bits of what might have once been food embedded in their piping. I could eat every meal at restaurants, if I so desired, and I didn't have to cook at all if I didn't want to. I could decorate as I saw fit and change my decor anytime I liked. I didn't own my home, so if something broke I could call the landlord. I worked hard and I played hard. Even though a small part of me thought maybe I should settle down, I came to a place of total peace as a single gal. I stopped looking for Mr. Right and decided I was perfectly fine without him.

Then I met a man, fell in love, got married, and had a baby. Just like that. My friends were shocked. My family was shocked. I was shocked. I guess everyone expected me to stay single forever. I guess no one, including me, could envision That Girl being a Mom. The first six months of being a wife and mother, we were living in Pittsburgh in a two-bedroom apartment outside of town. My husband was working with a man I loathed and I had no friends at all. My life had taken a U-turn so sharp I was in a state of total shock. Here I was, married and totally overwhelmed with being the caregiver for a small, mewling, needy human being. I cried. Often. Rivers, oceans, seas of tears. My life had become an endless blur of nursing, diaper changes, and baby talk. I was lucky if I could take a shower most days. I went from high heels, garter belts, and slinky dresses to overalls, nursing bras, and sweatpants overnight.

I didn't have a creative outlet, or any outlet at all. I had no support system of women to show me what you're supposed to do with a baby when you must take a shower, or go to the bathroom, or talk on the phone. I had no one to explain how to know when to call the doctor or when to let it ride. I had no one to watch the baby while I went out for a cup of coffee or a stroll down the sidewalk for a moment of relief from the monotony of caring for an infant 24/7.

Sometimes I handed the baby off to my husband and left. Where are you going? I don't know. When will you be back? I don't know. When I feel like I can do this without screaming.

I didn't know why other women didn't tell me the truth. Why didn't someone explain how hard it was? How isolating it was? How stressful it was?

Can a woman be a mother and still have a room of her own? I surely tried, but I can't say that I always succeeded.

My child has ventured forth into adulthood, and I have new challenges to face. It seems as if That Girl is a million miles away. She's faded into the rearview mirror, replaced by the face of an aging woman. That Girl is a distant memory, along with her tight ass and her saucy, naughty, carefree attitude. I find it hard to believe she was ever me. Yet, she stares back at me, defiantly, from faded photographs.

I miss That Girl. I wish she'd come for a visit sometimes. I wish it were possible to have all that I have now and still be That Girl on occasion.

I think every woman needs to revisit That Girl sometimes.

AGING DISGRACEFULLY

The older I get, the less certain I am that I have any of the answers. I can barely remember the questions. What was I talking about again? Oh, yes, life after 50. There is life after 50, as evidenced by my ability to type this sentence. There's more than that, though! There's so much more! It's not all vaginal lubricants, saggy breasts, and vitamin supplements. Even if you didn't plan well and save a nest egg (not that I'd know about that), there are places to go and people to see. Adventures await.

Sure, the rest of the world wants you to slow down, but why let that hold you back? This is the perfect time to speed up. The next time people offer sage advice on why you need to age gracefully, feel free to remind them that how you age is none of their damn business.

In that spirit, here are seven arguments for aging DISgracefully from a woman who knows a thing or two about it. Feel free to borrow them as needed, and discard any that don't work for you.

1. BOTOX

It's not just the deadliest substance known to man, it's what's in my forehead. Don't approve? I'd get upset, but I can't make angry faces anymore.

2. WINE

Let's hear it for wine! It's what's for dinner! It also keeps me from running off naked and screaming into the wilderness. Plus, it's filled with antioxidants, so it's a win-win. Don't even think about taking my wine away. If you think I'm crazy now, you should see me without it. Or not. Probably not. Did you hear? You can buy wine in a box now! What a wonderful time to be alive.

3. HOTNESS

It's true, I'm not as hot as a 20-year-old. I'm much hotter. I'm also sweaty, sleepless, and bitchy. You have a problem with that?

4. WRINKLES

Those aren't wrinkles—they're the sum total of my life experiences. A map without lines won't take you anywhere, least of all anywhere interesting.

5. GRAY HAIR

Why do we call it gray hair? It's not gray. Gray is such a dull color. It's platinum! It's silver! It's the color of moonlight, magic, and ice!

6. AARP

Dear AARP, I'll retire when I'm damn good and ready. One more invitation in my mailbox and you will be seriously sorry. Send it with a free membership to the Wine of the Month Club, then we'll talk.

7. ECCENTRICITY

There is a distinct difference between being crazy, bizarre, and eccentric. It is mostly measured by the amount of money in your bank account and your personal presentation. I am not crazy. I am borderline bizarre, but striving daily toward eccentricity. Here's to the journey.

You don't really need any excuses for aging disgracefully—it's your prerogative. After surviving everything that's brought you past the midcentury mark, you've earned the right to age in whatever manner you choose. Dive on in, sister, the water's fine! Wear whatever damn bathing suit you please, or skinny-dip if that's your thing.

One of the joys of aging is that our priorities change. We lift our gaze. We are freed from the pressure to be pretty. We realize that in all those years we spent worrying about what people were thinking about us, people mostly weren't thinking about us at all. That's a powerful revelation. We aren't disappearing, we're being given an opportunity to resonate on a higher frequency.

STOP SMOOTHING WRINKLES

Women have this thing we do. It's our defense mechanism. It's how we manage to get up and get moving, even when life is so unbearable that we'd rather crawl back into bed and live on wine in a box, ice cream, and cheese puffs. This thing we do is a combination of smoothing wrinkles and erasing rough edges with a heavy side dish of frantic denial. It's a primal ache, a deeply rooted need for order in chaos and light in darkness. It can be a good thing, it really can. But sometimes I think we miss out on the richness of things because we're in such a hurry to run from the hard stuff.

I think it's okay to embrace the wrinkles, run our hands along the rough edges, and dive deep into the sorrow until we swim our way to the other side. I think there is a value in letting go of the need to control everything and letting life happen without judging or racing in to fix it.

NOT EVERYTHING NEEDS to be fixed. It's okay to be sad and to rest with that until we feel happy again. We just need to leave a trail of cheese puffs so we don't get lost in there.

If cheese puffs aren't your metaphorical thing, feel free to insert a snack treat that works for you.

But I digress. The mantra is "It's okay. I'm okay. It's all going to be okay." It's a good mantra. Still, there are aspects of being a woman over 50 that aren't okay. It's good to say that out loud, and to give other women over 50 the permission to do the same. Things feel less insurmountable when you realize that you're not alone. So much of the denial of the truth holds women back.

I rarely talk about menopause or aging with my female friends. It's not that we aren't all struggling through it, because we are. We just don't know how to talk about it. The few times I've opened that can of worms on social media, the comments have been very enlightening. You get sympathy from women who are suffering similar problems, or advice from women who will explain that you're doing it wrong, or absolute denial from women who have no idea what you're talking about because everything is fine and dandy in their neck of aging town. Take this supplement! Try this diet! Do yoga! Try harder! You're doing it wrong!

I've been shushed, shamed, accused, and blamed for talking about weight gain, mood swings, difficulty finding work, ageism, sexism, hot flashes, and chiskers. "Good grief, don't talk about that, in public! What's wrong with you?" Much like the deep secrecy that surrounds puberty, periods, and pregnancy, there's a code of silence that surrounds menopause and aging.

I'm not going to sugarcoat it. Menopause can be misery. Becoming invisible is fucking frustrating. Being undervalued is maddening. Primal brain hardwiring is extremely difficult to circumnavigate. Men don't have to play by the same set of rules. Women over 50 are the most underemployed demographic. We are the least represented and the least served group by fashion, print, and digital media, and even pharmaceutical companies. Most of these things are managed by men, who have little understanding about what women want or need. Those are facts, but they are facts that can be changed. We have the power to change them. We can start telling the painful truth. We can stop smoothing wrinkles, stop making excuses, stop keeping secrets, and stop living in denial. Then we can begin the process of writing a new story that begins with rejecting the lies women believe.

LIES WOMEN BELIEVE

These are the lies that make us enemies, competitors, judges, and haters of ourselves and each other. These lies are ingrained in almost every aspect of our culture. We believe we will never be good enough because that is what we are told endlessly. These lies convince us to accept our inadequacy. Our driving force becomes fixing all of the things that are wrong with us, instead of embracing all that is right. It's the great distraction. We believe that we are less smart, less strong, less worthy, less beautiful, less powerful, and less important. After all, even the smartest, strongest women still get paid less, promoted less, and rewarded less. We are judged and in turn we judge ourselves and each other.

The lies don't stop when we are young, they continue to evolve as we age. We're told that being pretty and popular is what matters most when we are young. We're told that having babies and being a "good wife and mother" is what matters most when we are fertile. We're instructed to fade away when we reach maturity.

> **WOMEN'S INSECURITIES ARE,** after all, a
> driving force of much of the world's economy.
> We spend half of our lives feeling inadequate,
> and the other half becoming invisible.

The media and the makeup, fashion, home decor, and weight-loss industries perpetuate the lie that we are not good enough. We are told that an endless array of shiny new things will make us better, because we will never be good enough on our own. Women's power is so threatening that it has been systematically undermined for centuries. It's a tricky thing, because the desire for beauty, love, acceptance, and connection is intrinsic to being human. The opposing lie—that we should not sparkle, not shine, not seek attention, and not make ourselves look on the outside as Technicolor as we feel on the inside—is just another version of the same tired story. The lie is the same: We are not enough. The lie keeps perpetuating, expanding, evolving. The lie must persist; we must keep reaching for the golden ring as we go around and around on the pretty horses. Without the lie the carousel stops and the whole façade cracks.

Wait, what? That lipstick is not going to make me beautiful? Those new pants aren't any better than those old pants? That throw pillow is not going to change my life? That diet is not going to make me happy? That magical cream is not going to fix all my problems? That cell phone is not going to make me cool?

Then comes social media, with its heady allure. Look at me! Look at me! I took another selfie! I bashed a celebrity! I shared a picture of a puppy! I like purple! I bought some shoes! Do you like me? Do you think I'm good enough? Thumbs-up! Share! Comment! Yay! It's seductive, it's distracting, it's debilitating. Just keep looking for meaningless validation while we mine your data and offer it to the highest bidder.

As long as women keep believing the lies, as long as we remain distracted, we'll be so busy chasing things with no substance there won't be time for finding the substance within ourselves and others. If we're not good enough, obviously no one else is. So we'll be sure to drag them back down if they forget. The lies keep us disconnected, they keep us from rising to our potential, they keep us on the carousel.

As long as we live our lives in search of acceptance from a world that deems us "less than," we will never become greater.

WHAT WOMEN OVER 50 WANT

Yesterday I was chatting with my neighbor. He asked me what I do. I explained that I do a variety of things, including hosting videos, making TV appearances, writing, blogging, designing, and consulting. He expressed surprise that I worked in TV. I explained that I appeared on air at a home shopping network for 11 years, but jokingly suggested I'd aged out of that job.

He laughed, looked me right in the eye, and said, "Well, older women want to see beautiful women on TV. They don't want to see old women."

I paused, and thought to myself, "Did he seriously just say that to my face?"

Another man telling another woman what women over 50 really want. I have heard variations on this statement countless times from countless old and usually not even remotely hand-some men, who seem convinced they have a special bead on what older women want.

Screw you and your antiquated, ageist, sexist, boring beauty standards. How dare you stand there and look me in the eye and suggest that I'm not beautiful because I'm over 50. I did not let my neighbor's comment slide past me without a response.

I calmly and firmly replied, "I am beautiful. I am their cus-tomer. Women over 50 want to see themselves reflected on TV, in film, in magazines, and in advertising. We don't want a 20-something beauty queen with baby smooth skin talking to us about wrinkle creams."

I would like to report that he apologized. He did not. He stared at me slack-jawed and uncomprehending.

The truth is, it is men who want to see young women on

magazine covers, in movies, on TV shows, and in advertising. Men are hardwired to be attracted to women who are fertile. Since men make most of the decisions and create most of the content, most of what is served to us is a parade of pretty, young women. When women create the content and make the decisions, the message is very different.

This is the fallacy upon which most of the current marketing and product development and content creation for women of a certain age is built. It's a shitty foundation that lacks merit and substance. It is often so far off the mark it is baffling.

Yes, I'm pissed. I'm tired. I'm aching for someone to stop talking and to start listening.

My thoughts, my feelings, my opinions, my dollars count.

Ask me, ask us, listen to us. We know what we want and it's not what we're getting. We want to spend our money, so help us help you.

I have never been one of the "beautiful people," but I have always felt beautiful. I have always known that true beauty shines from within. I'm not immune to the charms of the "beautiful people," but I'd also like to see a generous helping of interesting people who reflect the endlessly fascinating, beautiful variations of being. I want to see myself reflected in the media. I want to challenge the current beauty standards and turn them upside down. I am not alone. I want to be able to picture myself wearing that outfit, using that wrinkle cream, riding in that car, dancing in those shoes, making that jewelry, looking saucy in that dress . . . I want to be reflected as the vibrant, sexy, smart, BEAUTIFUL woman I am at this age and will be in the years to come. I want to be cherished, celebrated, and respected.

All women do.

FIFTY, and Other F-Words . . .

The Good	The Bad	The Ugly
FEMALE	FLATULENT	FRIZZY
FABULOUS	FOGGY	FUZZY
FEARLESS	FLUMMOXED	FRUMPY
FANTASTIC	FRAZZLED	FLOPPY
FORGIVING	FUNKY	FUNGAL
FOXY	FRAYED	FECAL
FEMINIST	FORGETFUL	FOUL
FECUND	FRAGMENTED	FEEBLE
FLAWLESS	FOOLISH	FOSSILIZED
FIERCE	FLIGHTY	FROZEN
FUN-FILLED	FATIGUED	FRAIL
FANCY	FLABBERGASTED	FEARFUL
FREE	FRUSTRATED	FORLORN
FRIENDLY		FORGOTTEN
FLUID		FAILED
FLIRTATIOUS		
FASCINATING		
FANTABULOUS		
FLAMBOYANT		
FORTUITOUS		
FULFILLED		
FUNNY		
FLEXIBLE		
FORTUNATE		
FORMIDABLE		
FEROCIOUS		

TWO

frazzled

WHAT TO EXPECT WHEN YOU'RE NOT EXPECTING ANYMORE

A woman is considered menopausal after she ceases having her periods for a year. Naturally induced menopause begins sometime in a woman's 40s or 50s. The average age for a woman in the United States entering menopause is 51. I entered menopause at the age of 48. It could not have happened at a crappier time. I was in the middle of the worst years of my adult life. It felt as if I'd been shoved off a cliff into an endless abyss of darkness. I filled my canteen with Sauvignon Blanc and held on for dear life. I was drowning in self-doubt, debt, and despair. I was also drowning in sweat. The sweat had started a few years earlier, and not a single doctor had answers as to why I was waking up in a puddle each morning. I'd moved so many times, I didn't have a long-term relationship with a lady doctor. My periods stopped. I was angry. I was morose. I began packing on the pounds at an alarmingly rapid rate. It wasn't pretty, people, not by a long shot.

I'm going to be really real now, because, as I said before, I think women should tell the truth. Some women float through menopause without a care. They'll wax poetic about how easy it was and how they survived by doing yoga and eating copious amounts of kale. The rest of us feel a deeply rooted urge to smack them senseless. There are lots of books about doing yoga and eating kale and navigating menopause with ease. This isn't one of them. That wasn't my experience, and it isn't most women's experience. This is my experience.

Welcome to *More Fun with Menopause*, our irregularly scheduled moment to contemplate the fun-filled symptoms of the pause that is meno!

I'd like to report that it's been a walk in the park for lo these past couple of weeks, when the wine wears off, the amount of dark chocolate needed for maintaining the status quo exceeds my body mass, escapist vacations fade into the mists of memory, and the herbal remedy Band-Aid™ bursts like a cork in the Hoover Dam after a flash flood, but I would be lying. It has been more like a crawl through gravel, in a heat wave, while being bitten by fire ants and pummeled with baseballs.

There are moments when I'm quite sure I'm functioning at 25 percent of my normal happy capacity. There has to be a word for that. Let's call it "happacity." My "happacity" is normally fairly high, mostly driven by an amazing gift for ~~forcefully shoving~~ gently placing those dark thoughts deep into the recesses of my subconsciousness. You know, denial. It's taken years of practice.

Based on the sad, sad confessional poetry I wrote in my 20s when I received the nickname "Madge," I have done a bang-up job of ~~deluding~~ convincing myself that I am generally a shiny, happy person. Most of life is perception; we become what we think. I grew weary of Depressing Feminist Poetry Madge. Besides, Sylvia Plath and Anne Sexton pretty much have that market cornered, and you know how well that worked out for them. I like Glittery Uplifting Madge better. I'm fairly certain the rest of the world concurs. Yet, stalwart, irreverent, Glittery Uplifting Madge is being sorely tested by the current fuzzy-brained, tear-filled fright fest being brought on by her rapidly depleting hormones.

In other words, my happacity is in the shitter, folks.

If Depressing Feminist Poetry Madge were to write something about this current state, it would read something like this:

Crawling out of my skin,
Though impossible,
Seems the only option.
Therefore the lack thereof
Leaves me lacking
A place to hide.
Who is this stranger
Inhabiting my body?
Can I coax her out with
Vague promises of
Dark chocolate and
Wine?

Glittery Uplifting Madge would write something like this:

Hang in there, Madge-y,
(Which rhymes with Vag-y)
See how I did that?
Auntie Flo is leaving,
Soon you won't be grieving.
This too shall pass!
No, really.
Just add glitter.
Lots and lots of glitter.

Will our plucky heroine find her happacity returning to above normal soon? How long will this emotional roller-coaster ride continue? Will regular use of an over-the-counter menopause remedy bring on brighter days? Is there enough wine in the world to keep her on the sunny side of the street? Stay tuned for the answers to these and any other questions that arise in the next episode of *More Fun with Menopause*.

I'm still free-falling, but I've grown more accustomed to the feeling. I've also found herbal solutions for most of the symptoms. They work well for around three weeks of each month, then, just like my cycles when I was menstruating, the fourth week is a crapshoot. Or more aptly, it's crap. Shoot me. During my most recent lady prodding, my lady doctor recommended that I wean myself off the herbal remedies. I was incredulous! Without the benefits of any hormone-level testing or discussing my symptoms and complaints, this female doctor suggested that I should suck it up and stop taking supplements. What amazes me is that not a single lady doctor I've visited for my annual lady prodding since entering menopause at 48 has discussed any form of hormone replacement therapy or any solutions at all for the symptoms. My complaints have mostly been met with shrugs. The underlying message is that women should suffer in silence. I believe there is a vast menopause conspiracy.

BILLIONS OF DOLLARS are spent researching, marketing, and promoting solutions for erectile dysfunction—a global crisis, apparently—but comparatively little money is spent researching, marketing, or promoting solutions for the symptoms of menopause.

I realize that not being able to get a boner is a tragedy, but not being able to function in your day-to-day life without wanting to run off into the woods screaming is a bit more challenging. I'm just saying.

CACTUS FLOWER

I have been dragging three cacti around for years. They were given to me to care for, and I've done my best, despite my brown thumb. They're barely hanging on, and only thrive in the summer months when they can sit outside and soak up the sunshine and raindrops. They're bedraggled and half dead, and I have counted them almost out many times. Yet, ever the stalwart fighters, they continue to surprise me. One cactus has grown a flower every year. This little cactus is half dead. Yet, somehow, it summons the will to form a stem and grow a flower that blooms for eight glorious hours. Weeks of anticipation, for eight hours of triumph.

I can relate to this little cactus. Sometimes I feel half dead, bedraggled, and lacking in sufficient sunshine and raindrops. There are days and even weeks when I think whatever hope I had of blooming again is delusion at best. Last week was one of those, and it was a doozy. I was down, out, and being pummeled relentlessly. It was tragi-comical, emphasis on "tragi."

There's a pattern of late: A seemingly wonderful opportunity appears out of nowhere! I get super excited about it!

"Hooray! New opportunity!" Take that, Failure.

Failure: "Not so fast, honey."

Then the new opportunity fizzles spectacularly.

Me: "Crap."

I toss up my virtual white flag and surrender.

"Okay, Failure. You win, I give up. I'm just a half-dead cactus in a crappy clay pot."

Resounding silence.

Me: "Whatever."

This morning, I woke up with a renewed resolve. I remembered that I'm not alone. There are millions of women like me. Our knowledge has value, our passion has not faded. We're not half dead, we're fully alive. Late bloomers bloom best, because we're survivors.

We've survived the unspeakable, we've navigated the impossible, we've been knocked down, shut up, and rejected over and over again. Yet, ever the stalwart fighters, we continue to surprise. We summon the will to form a stem and grow a flower even if it only blooms for a few hours. Then we do it again.

We may be counted out, but we're only out for the count if we refuse to get up and fight. We've got plenty of bloom left in us.

EVERYTHING YOU EVER WANTED TO KNOW ABOUT MENOPAUSE, BUT FORGOT TO ASK

What, exactly, is menopause? Well, first there's perimenopause. Perimenopause is triggered by the decrease in the production of the hormones estrogen and progesterone. Perimenopause begins several years before the cessation of menstruation. As your estrogen and progesterone levels fluctuate, you experience physical symptoms. Menopause begins when menstruation ends, and once you are a year into menopause, you're officially post-menopausal. That said, the symptoms can continue long after you have reached post-menopause.

Beyond the cessation of the ability to conceive a child, a woman's body changes in myriad ways. Everyone is different, but here's a fun-filled overview of what happens to a woman's body when the production of these hormones is decreased enough to trigger menopause. You may experience some of these things, all of these things, or none of these things, in which case, go eat some kale and leave the rest of us alone.

- Menstruation ceases. I think we can all get behind that initiative.
- Your vagina dries up. This makes sex challenging, thus the lady lubricant market.
- The fluid that has left your vagina takes refuge in your tear ducts.
- Your bladder goes on strike. This makes sneezing, laughing, and coughing rife with potential for embarrassing leakage, thus the adult diaper market and jokes about older women peeing themselves.
- Sleep becomes elusive. You may find it difficult to fall asleep or find yourself waking up every hour or so staring at the ceiling. Lack of sleep will contribute to your rapidly declining enthusiasm. Whee.
- Sex, well, it's complicated. For some women the libido exits stage left, for others it goes on overdrive. The good news is that accidental pregnancy is no longer a concern. There's something upon which we might hang our cervical cap.
- Your mood swings rival Jack Nicholson's in *The Shining*.

- You experience the hot, wet excitement of night sweats. It might be a good time to stock up on rubber sheets and terry-cloth pajamas.

- You run out of enthusiasm regularly due to lowered energy levels. Coffee will become your new best friend as you and Juan Valdez begin a steamy affair.

- Your belly bloats, making you feel like the saddest float in the Macy's Thanksgiving Day Parade.

- You are introduced to the joys of foughing and faughing. This is the combination of a fart and a cough or a fart and a laugh. These often happen in rapid succession. It's especially fun in public, like, say, in the cereal aisle at the grocery store. Fough, faugh, repeat. Follow up with jazz hands—it adds a little something extra to the performance.

- Your bowels revolt, making processing last night's dinner an ongoing challenge. We'll call this New Adventures in Digestion, because at least it sounds like fun.

- Your skin starts itching an itch that no scratch can alleviate.

- Mood swings are soon joined by irrational, debilitating anxiety. This is most likely to arise in the wee small hours of the morning when you are wide awake and staring at the ceiling. This creates a phenomenon I call "brain spinning," whereupon you obsess over things you cannot change. This can go on for hours, and is best alleviated by getting up and watching TV. This is how the home shopping industry was built.

- Your waistline, left unchecked, expands in direct proportion to your shock and awe. I recommend stocking up on stretchy pants.

- Your pores expand to the size of small craters. You find yourself eyeballing spackle with renewed excitement.

- Your bones become brittle. You will give them new nicknames like snap, crackle, and pop.

- Your heart becomes vulnerable in more ways than one.

- Your skin begins to wrinkle and sag, thus the multimillion-dollar magical cream market. You'll wonder who that wrinkled, saggy old woman is in your mirror. It's you. Surprise!

- Your face loses volume as underlying facial fat disappears. This is what leads aging actresses to overfill their faces with silicone in a futile attempt to regain their youth. There's a procedure that involves taking fat from your posterior, processing it in a centrifuge, and injecting it into your face to restore volume. Yes, your face will look like your ass, but in the best way possible!

- Your neck becomes unrecognizable. You'll start considering the logic of turtlenecks in August and stocking up on decorative neck scarves. See chapter 5.

- You feel as if your entire body is on fire while raging hot lava is pumped into your veins, rolling up from the tips of your toes to the top of your head. This is called a hot flash, which is a misnomer. It's not a flash, it's more like a firing squad.

- Your hair begins to go thin on the top of your head, usually toward the front, making it impossible to hide. Fret not because new hairs will begin to appear on your chin to divert attention away from your thinning hairline. What fun! I call them chiskers (short for chin whiskers) and I hate them. Fuck you, chiskers.

- Your feet dry out, your toenails thicken, your fingernails thin, and the backs of your heels crack and peel. Pedicures move up to the top of your to-do list.

- Your skin thins, turning seams on socks and tags on garments into torture devices.

- Your brain abandons you at crucial moments.

Menopause: More fun than a barrel of vaginal lubricant! Sign me up! Wait, don't. Shit, someone already did.

Basically, menopause is the flip side of puberty. Back then, you were feeling the overwhelming rush of hormones and now you're feeling the overwhelming angst of their departure. I'd like to take this moment to award my stalwart husband a prize for surviving the dual assault of puberty and menopause. Yes, my daughter and I went through the change together. I'm still changing, but she's made the leap into womanhood. We all survived mostly unscathed. Mr. Potter has managed to maintain a sense of humor and much of his sanity. I believe this was achieved by the judicious use of headphones and extended walks with the dogs.

The thing is, no one seems to care very much about menopause, or menofuckingforever as I like to call it. It's a lady problem, and you know how that goes. It's also an old lady problem.

This means we need to keep that shit to ourselves. We are expected to suffer through it silently, just as we suffered through puberty, PMS, periods, pregnancy, and childbirth. Keep your chin up, darling. Have another glass of wine. It's not a big deal. Yet, it is a very big deal when you are attempting to deal with it and deal with the logistics of day-to-day life while maintaining the appearance of sanity.

But your experience does not have to be the same as my experience. You do not have to suffer silently. You can arm yourself with information. You can demand solutions. You do not have to participate in the great capitulation. There are days when I feel like running away and joining the circus, and days when I feel like I've got this under control. I just keep putting one foot in front of the other. It gets easier with every step. It helps to reach out to other women who are on the same path and share the road for a while. It helps to laugh at the absurdity of it all, especially when you feel like crying. It helps to scream into a pillow on occasion. Eventually, the good days outnumber the bad. It gets easier. It took some effort, but I found my groove and I'm making my way to the other side, and you can too.

THREE

forlorn

REIMAGINING THE EMPTY NEST

MOM

If you had told 25-year-old Margot that she would be married with a child at 34, she'd have laughed out loud. While I was in graduate school in Pittsburgh, I met the man who would become my husband. At the time, after a series of unfortunate relationships, I was not in the market for a significant other. Yet, something about him caught my fancy and soon we were dating. A year later, we were married, new parents, and moving to eastern Pennsylvania to open our own business. Eighteen years later our daughter, Avalon, started her freshman year in college. I never imagined that I could love anyone as much as I love my child. She is my best creation, by far. She continues to delight me on a daily basis. She's my best friend, my favorite flavor, the sprinkles on my ice cream, the peanut butter to my chocolate. We're so much alike it's scary, yet different enough to find myriad reasons to disagree about virtually everything.

Being a mother is one of the hardest jobs on the planet. Your mission is to raise your children, equipping them with everything they need to thrive without you. You don't get time off for good behavior, you don't get sick days, and you don't get any medals for your sacrifices. Your heart has to open up completely, which means that when they leave it will crumble. I didn't know how difficult it would be. I was not prepared for the gaping hole my daughter's absence would leave in our home. Letting her go is the hardest thing I've ever done.

Had I known just how hard it would be to let her go, perhaps I'd have been more present, more mindful, more fully in the moment with her while she was growing up. I look back at summers spent frantically chasing book deadlines, or afternoons when she'd rush in from the school bus to tell me a story and I found myself torn between working and listening intently. I'm ashamed to say that work won out more often than not. You can't get those moments back. You can't get the moments of exquisite boredom back, either, though you realize in hindsight just how precious they were. I've done a lot of deep thinking over the past few months. I've battled the demons of regret. I did my best, after all, and that's pretty much all any of us can do. I've decided to cut myself some slack.

My wise friend Tamara once said, "Childhood is something you get over, like a bad cold." I think she's right on that one. My daughter knows she is loved. She's had plenty of my time, attention, and affection. Whatever indignities she's suffered by my less than perfect parenting have not crushed her hopes or dreams. As much as looking back may make us misty-eyed and romantic, the truth is most of us do our best as parents. We go into it with the best of intentions. We get it right some of the time and we get it wrong some of the time.

There's the romanticized, soft-filtered, greeting-card version of parenting, and then there's reality. Not every moment of raising children is a blissful, fun-filled, happy-go-lucky adventure. A lot of it is boring, exhausting, thankless, and unrelenting. Kicking ourselves for not parenting perfectly is absurd. Women constantly judge themselves and other women for not living up to impossible standards. I grew up in a time when kids played outside, all day long, and no one came racing after us to see what we were doing. I'm shocked that I survived childhood, considering the ill-advised nature of much of what my friends and I did together. Cries of "I'm bored" were met with sidelong glances and suggestions that we clean up our room or go play outside. I never doubted for a moment that I was loved, but I didn't expect my busy single mother to be a one-woman entertainment committee. I learned how to entertain myself. The idea that given another chance we'd relish every second is a faulty one. If your children have left you and successfully entered adulthood, give yourself a pat on the back. You did your job.

THE SUMMER OF FRANTIC DENIAL

I have been in a mostly uninterrupted state of blissful denial this summer. Blissful denial is not quite the truth. I've more honestly been in a state of frantic denial. There's been plenty of distraction from facing the empty nest. I've busied myself with TV appearances, packing, moving, unpacking, decorating, cleaning, and other domestic diversions. The day when my only child leaves for college is rapidly approaching. I am therefore savoring every delicious final moment. I've roped and wrangled her into all sorts of excursions to buy pillows, furnishings, and knickknacks. Any excuse for the two of us to slip away and enjoy an afternoon together is fair game. I don't feel even the least bit guilty about that.

What a gift she is, and what a joy it has been to raise her. What a smart, funny, thoughtful young woman she has become.

People seem to find some sadistic joy in reminding me that she's leaving. What is wrong with people? Can't they see that I'm barely holding it together? Insert sound of screeching tires and shattering glass here. I can sense it coming, as they exhale, look me straight in the eye with feigned concern, and ask, "What are you going to do when she leaves? How are you feeling?"

Seriously? How do you think I feel? I feel bereft. I feel heartbroken. I feel like the soft, cozy rug is being pulled out from under me. I feel like that fucking rug has been hiding an endless pit into which I might just fall. I feel like crap. This is going to be the hardest thing that I have ever done. This is going to make me feel unfathomably miserable. There are rivers of tears preparing to flow, damn it. She's going to be two hours away and it is going to feel like we're on different planets. We've had two practice runs at this, and she's horrible at staying in touch with us. Snapchat, you're my only hope!

She's my only child. There aren't any others waiting in the wings to distract me from the sadness just a little. I can't even begin to imagine what it will be like not having her here. I don't want to imagine it.

How am I feeling? I am feeling awful, quite frankly.

Thanks for asking.

I'm also feeling proud, excited, and deliriously happy for her. But those feelings don't dull the abject pain of facing the empty nest. Still, I signed up for this job 18 years ago, and this is part of the deal.

Here's to the Summer of Frantic Denial, the Fall of Sorrow, and the Winter of My Discontent. I'm holding out hope for the Spring of Thoughtful Refocus and, upon her most auspicious return, the Summer of Love.

EMPTY NEST SYNDROME OR THE
HOME GOODS® PROBLEM

According to Wikipedia:

> EMPTY NEST SYNDROME is a feeling of grief and
> loneliness parents may feel when their children leave
> home for the first time, such as to live on their own
> or to attend a college or university. It is not a clinical
> condition.

It is not a clinical condition. Therefore, they don't make a pill for
that. They do, however, make vodka, and for that I am grateful.
Note of caution: Empty nest syndrome can cause depression,
loneliness, identity crisis, marital conflicts, and alcoholism. Use
vodka sparingly.

The first rule of order: Take advantage of the new empty
room in your house. Rather than maintaining a shrine to your
not-so-wee one, take her departure as an opportunity to create
a room of your own. Virginia Woolf recommended it highly.
Man cave, schman cave, you need a lady room and, by golly,
you're going to get it!

I have discovered something disturbing. I'm not sure if this
is a nationwide epidemic, but here's how it played out for me.
While my husband and I were moving our daughter into her
dorm, we moved ourselves into a tiny apartment. I decided to
toss most of our old stuff that we'd been lugging around for the
past 18 years and start fresh. I was tired of looking at the same
old crap. I've been frequenting Home Goods on a regular basis
in search of new wall art and happy tchotchkes to perk up the

apartment. Since I work for myself and from home, my forays into civilization, which is a hike from Amish country where we currently live, happen during weekdays.

It goes something like this . . .

Drive to the Home Goods strip mall parking lot, and find a space that requires me to walk a little bit. I have a potent combination of crafter's and writer's butt, and I'm making small efforts to combat the further spread of my posterior. Grab oversized cart, muttering out loud to no one in particular that these carts are too freaking big. Steer oversized cart with obstinate wheels through undersized aisles. Wait impatiently for other shoppers to peruse the variety of items on the shelves while blockading aisle with oversized shopping carts. Mutter to self that people are rude.

Meander through the aisles in search of . . . je ne sais quoi. Begin to notice a frightening pattern. You are one of dozens of women over 50 in the store, with similarly glazed expressions, also searching for something. Realize that what you are trying to find isn't on a shelf. It's not in a box. It isn't tucked into a basket. What you are trying to find is a sense of purpose. What you are looking for is your mojo, which is most definitely not hiding under a decorative pillow at Home Goods. Fuck nuggets, how did that happen?

Still, this box of note cards that says "Hello, gorgeous" is oddly compelling. Toss cards into cart. This faux fur throw pillow just might be the solution to your dog hair problem! Yes! That globe, look at that globe! It's fabulous, isn't it? Shrugs from another shopper in aisle. Oh, maybe it's not that fabulous. Walk away, turn around to see that sneaky shopper sneaking globe into her cart. Feel a sense of deep loss at not scoring that fabulous globe.

Make your way to the shockingly long checkout line and peruse the impulse items on the shelves lining the aisle. Toss gummy raspberries into cart, seriously contemplate the need for candy-coated pumpkin seeds. Chat with other ladies in line amicably, except for that bitch who snagged your globe. She's dead to you. Give her meaningful side-eye glances.

Pay for your bag full of empty promises, shuffle back to your car. Feel an instant and insistent sense of ennui. Realize that you don't even like this stuff you just bought. Consider returning it for a moment, but decide it's not worth waiting in line and risking buying more stuff you don't need.

I discovered that we smart, independent, capable women over 50 are looking for something vital, something that makes us feel relevant. And though we're not sure, we think it might possibly be found on the shelves of a discount department store. Perhaps it's the notion that if we find the right combination of things our empty house will feel like a home again—or maybe we're trying to fill up the empty spaces in our hearts with enough knickknacks to make the pain go away.

AT SOME POINT you have to fill up the empty spaces with new experiences, not new stuff. That means getting up off your sassy ass, wiping those tears away, and marching bravely forward into your future. Or, start the car and head to Target®, because maybe that's where your mojo is.

OH, HELLO, IT'S YOU AGAIN

My husband and I are still adjusting to being together all day several days a week. We both work from home when my husband isn't out of town for work. When our daughter was here, she served as our buffer. Now that our buffer is gone, it's just us. Oh, hello, it's you again.

I'm loud. I'm annoying. I talk to myself. I make up songs and sing them loudly and repeatedly. I curse at my computer and inanimate objects as if I suffer from Tourette syndrome. I don't suffer from Tourette syndrome, but I may have a previously undiagnosed condition I've dubbed Rampant Potty Mouth syndrome. I'm setting up a charity, your contributions are deeply appreciated. Fuck yeah, let's do this!

My husband has the patience of a saint, but even saints have limits. The prevailing wisdom regarding Empty Nesters is that it is a time for couples to reconnect and explore their relationship without their children.

Last week, we were in the car driving to the grocery store and my husband said, "I just figured out what's wrong." "What is it?" I asked. "I miss our kid," he said, with a deep sigh.

Yeah, me too.

My first frenzied response to surviving the Empty Nest syndrome was to start a blog called Cocktails Cupcakes Crafts. I made plans for my husband and me to visit local makers of said aforementioned "C" words. So far, we've visited an artisanal alcohol distillery and a French bakery. My husband is not keen on further explorations, as the first two cost us just under $100. I've been crafting up crazy cocktails and baking all manner of decadent desserts. I've stocked up the cupboards and fridge with flour, sugar, chocolate chips, key limes, Meyer lemons, heavy cream, and a variety of sprinkles and colored sugars. Though my aforementioned oversized posterior is a serious concern, I figured I'd roll with it. Life is short, eat dessert. That's the new mantra.

Well, it was the new mantra, until we were at the grocery store last week. My husband announced matter-of-factly that he's considering giving up alcohol, carbohydrates, and sugar.

God help me.

Upon further reflection and after regaining the 10 pounds I had recently lost, I decided that the blog sounded much better on paper than it did in reality. It was just another thing that demanded attention, perfection, and time. Sure, making cocktails, cupcakes, and crafts was fun, but not when it was compulsory, a daily directive that was, in the end, just another distraction. I dialed it back a little, and now I only make cocktails, cupcakes, and crafts when the mood strikes. Much better!

We're still finding our sea legs on this new adventure together, redefining who we are and who we are to one another. My husband travels for work when he isn't working from home. We're suddenly apart more than we've ever been before, and it's been a challenge for both of us. It has not been as difficult for him, and that's been difficult for me. I've had to pull him away from a tendency to turn inward, ask him to focus outward a little more. I've also had to pull myself away from a tendency to focus outward, and turn inward to find out who this new me is and what makes her excited to get up every day. We're rediscovering ourselves and each other, remembering who we were before we were parents, charting new territory, together, again.

Oh, hello, it's you again! Hooray!

THINGS TO DO

Looking for things to do now that the kids are gone? Fret not—we've got you covered!

- Kids left home? Feeling lonely? Stalk them on social media! It's easy and fun! Don't bother with Facebook, they're not there. Get a Snapchat account and give yourself a mysterious code name like StalkMuch or NotYourMom. They'll never guess it's you.

- Use your free time to devise new ways to make your child feel guilty for not keeping in touch. Emails! Tweets! Texts! Facebook Posts! Instagram photos with captions like "Wish you were here, but you're not and you never call. #sadface." and "Contact me if you see this child. #lonelymom."

- Turn their old toys into complex sculptures and sell them at your local modern art gallery. Give them serious names like "Crap my kids broke 10 minutes after they opened it" and "This is where my money went" or "Sharp things I peeled off the bottom of my feet."

- Rent their room on Airbnb®.

- Take up yoga. Re-envision your kid's room as a serene escape from the frenzy of daily existence. Decorate it with vaguely Asian-influenced artifacts. Realize that yoga looks exhausting after watching a series of yoga videos. Re-envision your yoga studio as a cocktail lounge. Pour yourself some vodka and smile serenely while chanting, "Om, yes I like this drink."

- Convince your spouse to join you on misbegotten adventures while doing research for your new blog. Call it something kicky like Xanax® and Birkenstock® or Desperately Seeking My Jawline.

- Take up nudism. Scare the shit out of the UPS guy when you forget to grab your robe before answering the door. Wave goodbye serenely while sipping your vodka. Your work is done here.

SEXY TIME

Suzanne Somers wrote a book a few years back called *The Sexy Years*. She is a proponent of hormone replacement therapy. She claims it will restore your youth and your libido. If I could afford it, I'd gladly give it a whirl. My libido disappeared about the same time that Auntie Flo took off for parts unknown and my happacity hit the shitter.

This is me being really real, folks. We're letting it all hang out here. Oh where, oh were has my libido gone? Oh where, oh where could it be? If you see it, please direct it to my lady parts. Thanks.

When I pitched this book you are reading, I initially had an entire chapter slated for discussing sex after 50. As you can see, I don't have a chapter's worth of thoughts on that topic. Forgive me. Lots of ladies have lots of sex after 50, so please don't despair. I'm just one lady. I'm not the only lady not feeling the tingle in her nether regions after 50, but that's okay. You don't have to give up! Get some of that yam cream and get on with it, girl!

The loss of my libido has also made me feel less excited about the constant onslaught of soft porn on cable TV shows. Good God, I'm becoming a prude. Or am I? Is it just me? I feel like the sex in these shows is so graphic, so banal, so rudimentary, and more than occasionally violent and lacking in romance. The shock value is lost, because it's not shocking anymore. Let's be honest: Real sex is not pretty. I know people do it, but I don't wish to observe.

It's hard to feel sexy when the prevailing narrative strongly implies that you are no longer sexually appealing. Not that I'm blaming the narrative, mind you, but it isn't helping the story line. As I've mentioned before, biologically speaking, my need to procreate is no longer primal. My need to be touched, caressed, cherished is still there. It's just not being met with affirmative action from my hormones.

I can't offer advice on sex after 50, since I am not having much of it. If feeling sexy after 50 is important to you, then make it your mission to figure it out. Now that my daughter is away and my husband and I are home alone, perhaps we will figure it out, too. Meantime, the irony of finally having the freedom to be sexy whenever we please coinciding with the unceremonious departure of desire is not lost on me, much the way the ability to sleep in has been countered with my circadian clock chiming a 6:30 a.m. wake-up call each morning. There is a lot of irony in aging, isn't there?

All hope is not lost. We still have love and laughter and friendship—and passion that has not gone forever; it's just on hiatus. Our sexy time will come again. Pun intended. Wink, wink, nudge, nudge.

Come on, ladies, we have to laugh at this shit or we'll cry.

FOUR

flexible

CHANGING
CAREERS
MIDSTREAM
WITHOUT
DROWNING

OVER 50 AND UNEMPLOYED

I like to reinvent myself every 10 years or so. This is my story, and I'm sticking with it. I've also been telling myself for years that I'm a late bloomer. This is how I have made myself feel better about not quite having reached the brass ring of success. It's called delusion. It's a handy way to increase your happacity. The goal for late blooming was 50. Therefore, at 55, I'm a few years behind schedule. I'm going to go ahead and push that back to 70.

That feels much better. I can feel my happacity increasing exponentially.

The past seven years, as I approached and then crossed over into my 50s, have been filled with painful lessons in self-belief and tenacity. After what would best be described as my year from hell, and the PTSD that followed, one seemingly fabulous opportunity after another has appeared and disappeared like a pea in a frustrating shell game.

I feel like a river stone. The excess has been worn away. The essence is being revealed.

It used to be that people had a career for a lifetime, working for the same company until retirement. I have never followed that career path, and many people I know who did found themselves shocked and unemployed when the economy tanked and jobs started moving overseas. Then tech boomed and age and experience were considered liabilities. It's an interesting time to be over 50, and it gets more interesting as time marches forward. By *interesting* I mean challenging and fraught with peril. I'm convinced that the best way to survive and thrive professionally after 50 is to work for yourself. Multiple income streams will help keep you from becoming dependent on only one source of income and therefore put you in less jeopardy of ruin if that one source disappears. I don't see myself retiring, at least not in the usual sense. I like working, feeling productive, doing things every day. It gives my life purpose. I also like having enough money to pay the bills, and since a series of professional missteps and time out of the full-time workforce have led me to a place where I have no significant nest egg, I'm going to have to keep working until I save up enough money to do otherwise, and I'm okay with that.

While I was researching this book, I found a disturbing number of articles on the same topic—the employment trends for women over 50. If you are a woman over 50 seeking work, I have some bad news for you. The prevailing wisdom says that many women over 50 have "spotty work experience" because they have spent too many years out of the workforce raising children. I think this is a crock of doody. Being a stay-at-home mom is one of the hardest jobs on the planet. How absurd to think that mothers are not employable—they have a litany of skills! I would argue that they're far better equipped to handle the demands of today's workforce than most, due to the variety of challenges they've faced raising children. I think we should get more creative about our resumes.

CODE WORDS FOR FORMER STAY-AT-HOME, OR WORK-FROM-HOME, MOM SKILLS

- Spent years driving children around? Chauffeur and/or Race Car Driver

- Helped with homework? Tutor

- Scheduled endless appointments and wrangled lessons, practices, performances, and play dates? Personal Assistant

- Navigated the complexities of toddler logic? Child Psychologist

- Entertained children after an endless chorus of "I'M BORED"? Cruise Director

- Decorated your home on a budget? Lifestyle Expert

- Whipped up enough meals for picky eaters to feed the population of a midsize country? Master Chef

- Endured teacher conferences, visits to the principal's office, and PTA meetings? Hostage Negotiator

- Brokered complex peace treaties between screaming siblings? Secretary of State

- Mastered the art of the last-minute science project? Chief Creative Officer

- Consistently balanced the household budget? Chief Financial Officer

- Been a Stay-at- or Work-from-Home Mother for over 20 years? Chief Executive Officer

The sad truth is that women's work has never been valued. Even women who have been in the workforce full time, or women who have never had children, find their options shrinking after a certain age. This is part of the ongoing theme of becoming invisible. It's also part of the ongoing theme of treating women like second-class citizens. Women in the workforce are paid less than their male counterparts, are less likely to be promoted, and are more likely to be the victims of sexual harassment. All of these inequities are statistically more pronounced among people of color.

There is a mostly unspoken idea that to become successful a woman must be of questionable character. Even the most successful women suffer from this prejudice, just ask Hillary Clinton. Sexism is alive and well, and when it mingles with ageism it's a potent combination. If a woman has children and she's successful, she has neglected her children. If a woman doesn't have children and she's successful, she's selfish. If a woman has climbed the ladder of success, she's done it either on her back or at the expense of other people. How could any woman succeed by virtue of her intellect, talent, vision, hard work, and skill? That's preposterous!

An archaic idea undergirds the manner in which women are treated in the workforce: Men are the main breadwinners and therefore they deserve to earn more money and more promotions. Even if that belief is no longer true, it affects women in the workforce every single day.

The bottom line is that the value of women's work is ranked below that of men—at any age—and women workers over the age of 50 are viewed as particularly disposable. This pisses me off, and it should piss you off. If it pisses us all off enough, maybe we'll start making some noise about it. If we make enough noise, maybe we can change this myopic belief.

LATE BLOOMER

A few years before I turned 30, while I was getting a degree in theater, a relative and I were talking at a wedding reception. I was explaining my plan to pursue my acting career after college. He paused, puffed on a cigarette, stared at me incredulously, and said, "Aren't you a little long in the tooth for that career?"

I wasn't quite sure how to respond to that question.

Really? Not even 30 and all hope was lost? I had not even stopped to consider that perhaps I was too old to pursue acting. It was and still is my passion to perform, and I did it well. It was my sole and driving force, the reason I got up every day and hit the ground running. I couldn't imagine not performing. I surely couldn't imagine changing direction and going to work in an office. It had not occurred to me that I wouldn't have a career as an actor.

Was I delusional? Perhaps. But I think a little delusion is required when navigating a dream that the world deems impossible.

I have never taken the easy road. I have never made safe choices. I have rarely done what was expected. I sometimes wonder how my life would look had I not chosen the road less traveled. Then I let that shit go because it's depressing as hell.

Here I am, at 55, after taking a hiatus to raise my lovely daughter, attempting the journey back toward what may well be the impossible, to make a viable career as a writer and an on-camera host and performer. I know people think I'm insane. I know people think any woman over 50 is insane for believing she has a future on camera or onstage. That is the age at which we are told to step aside and exit stage right. We are, after all, the older model. I am, literally, long in the tooth for this career. Yet, I don't think it's impossible. Improbable? Perhaps. But not impossible.

Recently, a friend and I were talking about my web show plans and she said, "Are you still pursuing that career?"

I was not quite sure how to respond to that question.

"Hell yes, I am. Why would I stop pursuing my passion? I'm just getting started!" I cried.

Yet, truth be told, that question has been rolling around in my brain ever since. Am I too old to pursue my dreams? Is it too late? Has that ship sailed? I thought I was taking a break, not tossing in the towel. I was on TV regularly up until a few months ago, after all. I was flown to LA by a big-three network recently to audition for a seat on a major new show. I have 15 years in live, unscripted TV under my belt and even more years onstage as an actor and vocalist. I just want to host and produce a web show and possibly pitch it to TV. Is that so wrong? Still . . . maybe . . . maybe all of these years of believing I actually can achieve the impossible have worn thin. Maybe from the outside looking in, I am that crazy person who refuses to give up on something that may have given up on her. Maybe I am immature and irresponsible. Maybe I need to grow up and get over it. Or maybe not. I am going with not. So there.

The craft career was a happy accident, the perfect solution for what to do to make a living while raising my daughter. I did it, it was fun, but I am ready to get back to my real passion. I never gave up on the performing career; in fact, I segued it into the craft career as often as possible. As I have never considered not doing what I love, I have no idea what I would do if I did something else. I am not sure if that makes me pathetic or determined. I don't know if that makes me full of moxie or full of shit. Like all things in life, it's about perspective. Obviously, I realize that the beauty part of my equation is on the decline. Yes, I can, if I can manifest the money, lift the neck and de-wrinkle the brow, but I also know that too much of that really isn't a good thing. You can only run from the crone for so long.

As ever, I say a heartfelt prayer to the Patron Saint of Late Bloomers, Mrs. Julia Child. If she could start on TV in her 50s, then, damn it, so can I. If a woman as unconventional and unlikely as Julia could become a television icon, then it is not impossible. Improbable, yes, but not impossible. I may fall flat on my face and look like a fool, but I'd rather fall from grace trying to attempt the impossible than give up on my dreams and crawl off into a cave to sulk. If that makes me crazy, so be it. I can't worry about what other people think about my choices. All I can do is keep marching bravely or foolishly forward.

THE POWER OF TENACITY

I have lost everything and started over five times as an adult. This is not an exaggeration. I have tried all manner of impossible things. I have failed spectacularly and lived to tell the story. Along the way, I have succeeded at a few of those impossible things. Most people would have given up and gone home long ago. I am not most people, but, then again, neither are you, unless you choose to be.

If there is one trait that has kept me from falling off the cliff of loss into a sea of despair, it is tenacity. The discovery of the power of tenacity came early for me. As a child, our little family lost everything and started over several times. That is not an exaggeration. I have been the "new kid" many, many times, even as an adult.

I am not going to lie—reinventing yourself can be exhausting. It does not get any easier as you get older. It is even more challenging, as a woman over 50, in a world that wants you to disappear. While most people my age have long abandoned their dreams, I am still in the ring. The stubborn refusal to stay down for the count, even when you're beaten, bloody, and bruised, is a testament to tenacity. The world may have counted you out, but the world does not get to decide your fate. You do.

If I have any wisdom to impart from the other side of the midpoint of my journey, it is this: Losing everything feels like the end of the world, but it is just the beginning of a new world. If you can let go of what you've lost, you can open yourself up to what might be gained. It's a choice. There is a certain comfort in mourning what was lost, and wrapping yourself up in that loss like a blanket. This allows you to avoid the second half of the experience, the journey back from the darkness into the light. It also keeps you from progressing, and it steals your joy.

I find directives like "Be Happy" to be lovely little affirmations that lack a key element. You can be happy, but in order to experience happiness you must take it. To take happiness requires releasing the things that keep you from opening yourself up to joy. You can't grab it if your hands are filled with sorrow.

THE GLASS IS not half empty or half full;
it's a vessel. You dip your cup into the
well and you choose what to drink.

You choose whether losing everything is the end of your story or the start of a new chapter.

MADGE'S ADVENTURE IN LA LA LAND

Three years ago, I was contacted out of the blue by a big-three network that was casting a new talk show. I thought it was a spam email at first. Before hitting the delete button, I decided to do some snooping around the internet to confirm it was real. Once I realized the mail was from an actual network casting agent, I hit reply.

The casting agent liked me on *Craft Wars* and found me again via the internet. I Skyped with him and the VP of Talent later that week. It went well. She said, "I LOVE YOU" about fifteen times. I was feeling pretty good about things. They offered to fly me in to LA for a shot at the last empty chair on the panel. What I didn't know was that there were hundreds of other folks, many of them big names that you would recognize, being vetted for this opportunity. These were people with teams of agents, lawyers, and managers, who had book deals, their own radio shows, product lines, and tons of experience appearing on network talk shows and TV commercials. Many of them were hosts of their own shows on cable TV. Two fashion industry icons were leading this panel, along with several other TV-savvy people, who had tons of time on camera and the confidence that comes along with that experience. This was what one calls "The Big Time."

They were looking for a mom who was a recognized expert in design, had on-camera experience, and who could also "keep it real." It became evident rather quickly that a regular mom, who was a few pounds overweight, a few notches too sparkly, and showing signs of her actual age was perhaps a little too real.

This is sort of crazy and perhaps I should have rethought this decision, but I showed up, on the first day, right from the airport with my hair in pigtails, wearing a giant quirky plastic necklace and a red gingham blouse that made me look more like an older Mary Ann from *Gilligan's Island* than a celebrity panelist. Lest you think me entirely daft, let me assure you that I had brought a far less kooky outfit to wear that day, but the flight arrived at LAX so close to the call time that I didn't have an extra minute to change. The casting agent had told me not to dress up or worry about being TV ready. So, I didn't. Derp. I should have remembered that the audition starts from the moment you walk in the door.

I arrived from the airport and dragged my suitcase up to the offices. I met the casting agent, who was delightful, and several other people on the team. I waited quietly on a bench until it was time for our group session. Our practice group included a ruggedly handsome young chef from NYC, who hosts a show on FYI now, but at that time was trying to break into the business; a southern woman who had a very popular movie written about her; a cable TV design expert from New Jersey (whose name escapes me, so she shall heretofore be known as Designing Woman); and a woman we shall call 53, who arrived just in time for our practice session, breathless and resplendent in an off-white leather jacket and designer heels.

Defying gravity and all logic, 53 looked amazing for her age (she was two years older than me at the time). Had she been 43, she still would have looked amazing for her age. She had the considerable benefit of many years of Botox, lasers, facials, and fillers. Her hair was swept up in an *I Dream of Jeannie*-style ponytail, and her neck and jawline were flawless. She told us that she practiced yoga, which was clear from the exquisite fit of her skinny-leg, dark-rinse blue jeans that just met the top of her crimson-soled designer stilettos. During rehearsal, she told a series of "sincere, heartfelt, touching" personal stories in a sultry Southern drawl, and with the perfect combination of smiling, pathos, and a smattering of teardrops. She laughed. She cried. She feigned sincerity. It was an impressive performance.

You can imagine how I felt, in my slightly wrinkled Mary Ann getup, next to the spectacular ageless beauty of 53.

The only note I made that day was to tone down my accessories.

The next morning, I woke up and got myself TV ready. This normally requires a small village, but lacking the budget for a beauty squad, I settled for a small village of one. Flagrantly ignoring the tone down directive, I wore an oversized necklace featuring clusters of giant cream faux pearls and sparkling crystals with matching earrings. I made the necklace, because I can DIY like that. I told myself that the host would appreciate my take-no-prisoners couture aesthetic. Once we arrived, we were escorted to the audition waiting room. It was packed with quasi-famous beautiful people, all buzzing with excitement over this opportunity. People in LA are not like the rest of us, they're all thinner, taller, and prettier. As I surveyed the room, recognizing many of the faces from network and cable TV, I started to think there must have been some mistake. What was I doing here? I was in way over my head. Sure, I was talented, but my resume consisted of 13 years on home shopping networks, one episode of *Craft Wars*, and two years appearing on a local TV station as a DIY expert. In short, it was a little thin, unlike my posterior. Still, I remained resolute. If they invited me to the table, I belonged there. As God was my witness, I was going to nail this audition.

Then they called our group: Me; a TV chef from the Bay Area, whom we'll call The San Francisco Treat; Designing Woman; and 53. Dammit. Impossibly, 53 looked even more flawless and confident than she had the day before.

We were escorted into a room with a panel of network execs sitting in front of a bank of cameras and lights. Standing in front of a long table was the host. She was tall. She was magnificent. She was even more gorgeous in real life than she looks in photographs. We will call her Fashionista. Fashionista was not fucking around. She sized us up quickly, gave us all big showbiz hugs and air kisses, as we duly marched to our assigned seats.

Fashionista spoke with the producers while we bantered with a male fashion stylist co-host, whom we'll call Mr. Style, and who "LOVE, LOVE, LOVED" 53's "high pony!" He did not, however, love anything about me. This was made evident by his complete disinterest. I conversed with the San Francisco Treat and let that shit go. I was going to nail this audition, bitches.

Lights. Camera. Action.

It was swift and mostly painless. Playing the "would have could have" game, I realize that I probably should have focused a little more on my area of expertise, in my responses. I also realized that my candid answers were so "everyday people"-focused that the other folks on the panel simply didn't understand what the hell I was talking about. When asked about my pet peeve, I bemoaned the drudgery of grocery shopping.

"Nobody likes grocery shopping, am I right?

"Don't you just hate it when you are waiting to grab a jar of peanut butter and the entire aisle is blocked for ten minutes while someone ponders their selection, as if the fate of mankind depended on it? It makes you want to start humming the theme from *Jeopardy*. And when did everyone start driving through the grocery store parking lot like it's the Indy 500? It's madness!"

The silence was deafening. I later realized that Mr. Style, The San Francisco Treat, 53, and Fashionista don't go grocery shopping in grocery stores. Designing Woman was no help at all, even though I'm certain she knew what I was throwing down. These people inhabit a totally different reality. Awkward.

Then came the moment when I knew it was over for me. In a flurry of dramatics and excess, 53 brought out her reading glasses to read a card that the host was holding. I have no idea where she was hiding those glasses, but my guess is in her bra because there were definitely no pockets in her pencil skirt and skintight sweater.

"Sorry, I can't see as well as I used to, it happens when you get older."

Fashionista asked, "How old are you?"

"Oh," she purred, pausing for full effect, "I'm 53."

Ta da.

Fashionista jumped up, raised her hand, and reached over the table so that she could high-five 53.

"YOU LOOK AMAZING!"

"I'm 51," I said mostly to myself.

Shrugs all around.

She really did look amazing for a woman with enough

money to maintain the appearance of youth. The host was right. However, for the record, I looked pretty damn good for a woman who does not have the money to maintain the appearance of youth and has had to rely instead on copious amounts of sunscreen, generous dollops of drugstore moisturizer, and a lot of creative visualization.

We were squired back to the waiting room. Five minutes later a woman came in and called off the names of the people who would be moving forward. 53 and The San Francisco Treat made it to the next round. Designing Woman and I had been cut. "Please collect your things and you'll be escorted to the lobby."

I proceeded along the walk of shame through the halls of the network, flanked on both sides by huge black-and-white photographs from some of my favorite TV shows through the years. I held back the tears and held my head high. I had been invited to the table, and that was something. A woman I shall call Tex Mex, who was known for her TV spots promoting a Mexican food–focused fast-food chain, and Designing Woman and I waited for the limo for what felt like an eternity. There is nothing worse than being rejected and not being able to make a clean getaway. Hey, Tex Mex got cut too. I was in good company. After what felt like an eternity, the limo arrived and whisked us back to our regularly scheduled programming.

When the show finally aired, it turned out they'd hired a twenty-something YouTuber, who was not a mom until mid-season. She made it to the second round, but 53 didn't make it all the way and neither did hundreds of well-qualified applicants. Fashionista quit the show two months into production.

It ended up being cancelled after the first season. I had dodged a bullet, which was a comfort, considering that I'd already relocated for a TV job that went awry, and the pay for the first year on the show was dismal.

That, folks, is show business.

WILL WORK FOR GLITTER

Countless times, over the years, I have been contacted by big companies asking me to do work for them. It usually starts out with an exploratory email in which they blow a lot of hot air up my skirt to elicit a response. I get these requests from all kinds of companies, most of them with plenty of money. They ask me to blog, make videos, create craft projects with step-by-step photos, make jewelry, appear on TV shows, consult, review, or write. You name it, I've been asked to do it. Some offer to pay me a pittance, some offer to pay me in glitter, some have offered to pay me and then forgotten that promise after the work was completed, and some offer to pay me with the elusive, intangible thing called publicity or exposure.

The pittance is at least an offer, if an insulting one. I will graciously thank them and respond with my fee schedule. On rare occasions, they will respond positively and we'll move forward. The glitter people really think that giving me free stuff is payment enough, and sometimes if the glitter is really fucking awesome, it is, but mostly it's just glitter. It piles up in the studio and no one will accept it as payment.

The thing that burns my biscuits is the incredibly insulting offer of free publicity. It goes something like this:

Dear Margot:
We think you are amazing! We love your [insert talent here] and would be honored to have you partner with us on our new initiative. Please contact us as soon as possible to discuss! We're excited to speak further.

Sincerely,
Possibly Delusional Person

Lately I am hitting the DELETE button more often, but occasionally I will bite.

Dear Possibly Delusional Person:
Sounds intriguing. Tell me more.

Cheers,
Madge

I keep my expectations low here; it keeps me from screaming and throwing things at my computer later.

Dear Madge:
We're thrilled that you're interested in working with us! We're huge fans! We are looking to partner with some of the biggest talents in [insert industry here] and we think you'd be a perfect fit. As you know, we have a huge following through our online platforms, subscriber lists, media outreach, yadda, yadda, yadda. We're looking for people like you to jump through hoops, work like dogs, give us your best and in exchange . . . wait for it . . . this is exciting . . . no, really . . . we will promote you to our considerable audience. Awesome, right?

Best,
Delusional Person

Dear Delusional Person:
It is not awesome. It is the opposite of awesome.
                    No.
                    Madge

I have worked for "publicity" for several big companies over the years. They made it clear that working for them for free (you know, for publicity) was a privilege and an honor and was going to be HUGE for my brand. I can count on no fingers the number of times that was actually true. None of it was huge for my brand. Every time I accepted that offer, I got nothing tangible in return. Oftentimes, it ended up costing me a pretty penny.

Working for publicity is like trading your cow for magic beans. Those magic beans sound good. I mean, gosh, they're magic, after all. Still, it doesn't take a rocket scientist to figure out that magic beans are just beans and that free publicity is almost always a false promise. I have had people expect me to pay for my airfare, hotel rooms, products to make things, and time away from my studio and family, and then react with incredulity when I suggested they should at the very least cover my travel expenses, if they really want me that badly. Not only did they expect me to provide work for "publicity," they also expected me to pay for the privilege of working for nothing.

The vague promise of future work, which I now avoid like the plague, has also been offered. One time, the producers of a TV show asked me to fly in on my own dime, and promised to have me back on the show when my first book was published, which they never did. A few years later they needed a last-minute on-camera fill-in on a side project. I agreed. I created over $500 worth of samples that their client refused to return, and for which I was never paid. Fool me once, shame on you, fool me twice, shame on me.

There was the big website that asked me to create a series of craft videos for "huge exposure." After spending $800 to make studio renovations, many hours making samples, and shooting the segments with a local camera guy . . . nothing. The producers disappeared. I have no idea what happened to the videos. Then a couple of years later they emailed me AGAIN with the same request. Seriously?

I have no one but myself to blame for all of the times I accepted less, because I'd convinced myself that the magic beans were different. They weren't. They aren't. They never will be different. I am NEVER working for magic beans or publicity again. I do not feel even remotely guilty for valuing myself enough to draw the line in the sand. I am worthy. I am exceptional. My talents have monetary value. I need to be paid in money. I am funny like that.

This is the kind of thing that regularly happens to creatives. There is a perception that if you make a living from your creative talents, you are doing it for fun—that you're not serious. There is a shocking lack of value placed on creativity. The sad truth is, there is an endless parade of creative people who ARE willing to jump through hoops for magic beans. They will argue endlessly that they have to start somewhere and it isn't their full-time job and they're doing it for fun and blah, blah, blah. Yes, we all have to start somewhere, how about we start by getting paid? If you aren't good enough to warrant a paycheck, you aren't ready to start a career as a creative. But the thing is, if you aren't good enough to warrant a paycheck, why are these big companies asking to work with you? Chew on that for a moment and see how it tastes. It's time we all stopped under-valuing our work because, until we do, the manufacturers, publishers, retailers, TV production companies, and magazines are going to keep expecting people to work for publicity or glitter.

Does the person writing the email work for publicity? Hell no.

We have to take a good hard look in the mirror and tell ourselves we are worthy. Because we are.

JOBS FOR WOMEN!

If you've been pounding the pavement looking for work, you know it's tough out there for a gal over 50. Don't worry, I've got you. Here are seven fabulous job ideas for women over 50:

1. Over 50? Becoming invisible? Now that your private parts are no longer in service, it's the perfect time to become a Private Investigator! You don't need a dick to be a private dick. How cool is that?

2. Bill yourself as an older nanny and market yourself as the perfect solution for women who don't want to worry about their husbands leaving them for a hot 20-something au pair. Call yourself Mrs. Doubtfree!

3. Are you a bossy bitch who likes to tell other people what to do? Do people love your "refreshingly real" advice and "take no prisoners" attitude? Do you enjoy kicking whiny, listless, unmotivated people in the ass with a steel-toed boot? Did you know that people will pay you money to do that? Yup, it's called Life Coaching, or being a Dominatrix. Six of one . . . Lace up your corset, grab that whip, and get on it, sister.

4. Want to lose all of your friends and isolate yourself from family members? Join an MLM (Multi-Level Marketing) company also known as a pyramid scheme. Post about the "amazing" products you're selling multiple times an hour on all of your social media accounts. Add everyone you know and even people you barely know to your virtual Facebook group without their permission. Soon you'll have drawers full of crap no one wants and plenty of time to spend with your cats. Win-win!

5. If you're crafty and you know it, raise your hand! Love to DIY? Live to craft? You can work in the craft industry as a designer and get paid in glitter and glue! That's right, companies are lining up to pay bloggers, designers, and video producers in currency they call exposure and free product! Sure, your landlord won't let you pay the rent in yarn, but think of all the fun you'll have! Similar opportunities await graphic designers, writers, photographers, caterers, and other creatives. What fun!

6. Speaking of fun, kids are fun, especially when they're not yours. Be a Rent-a-Grandma! Spend your days pumping children full of sugar; buying them toys that flash, squawk, and beep; and giving them heartfelt but outmoded advice that starts with the phrase "In my day," and sharing cautionary tales about ending up like their parents.

7. If all else fails, you can try your hand at selling crap on the internet. Everyone else is doing it. This is another effective way to use your social media prowess, and it's an excuse to hit thrift shops, yard sales, and flea markets. Think of it as a treasure

hunt and fancy yourself as a modern archeologist. Indiana Jones has nothing on you, girl. As you sift through the detritus of our toss-away society, you just might find a golden nugget. Or you just might find detritus. You'll never know until you try.

OWN YOUR FAILURE

If you're going to own your success, you must also own your failure. It's all part of the same story, after all. Everyone fails sometimes. The people who succeed the most have probably failed the most as well.

That's because they're the people who never give up, never back down, and never stop trying. They fail and fail and fail again until the rest of the world is probably thinking they're crazy or brilliant or perhaps a little bit of both. They aren't worried about the rest of the world. They're just picking themselves up, dusting themselves off, and starting again. They're not afraid to fail spectacularly because they know that's the only way they'll ever succeed spectacularly.

No matter how far you fall, keep climbing. If insanity is doing the same thing and expecting different results, persistence is pushing toward the same desired results differently. The law of averages is such that, eventually, if you try enough different approaches, you'll find the one that works. If no one is handing you the road map to success (because there is no road map), it's up to you to forge your way through the wilderness.

EVEN WHEN IT feels as if you're a failure, remember that you are not a failure, you simply haven't succeeded yet.

Keep marching bravely forward.

You must keep your sense of humor, because life is an absurdist tragicomedy and you are the star. Yes, you, sassy britches! What matters most isn't how many awards you win, or how many likes you get, or how many widgets you sell. What matters most is how much you love. I used to say it was how much you love and how much you are loved in return, but I don't think the return on the investment is the point anymore. We just love, because that is the point.

I am getting up every single day and believing that I can. What else can I do? I may own my failure, but I am also fully intending to own my success.

THINGS I SAID YES TO

When you work for yourself, you will find that other people do not value your time as much as you do. They'll assume that most of what you're doing is lounging around in silk pajamas, watching daytime TV, and sipping vodka. Sure, that may take up a large part of your day, but you need to set boundaries for the rest of the time when you're really working. If you don't, you will find yourself buried in things other people ask you to do. They'll fill up your dance card for you unless you take a stand. It's not easy, because women are programmed to say yes. We're people pleasers and wrinkle smoothers. Resist this programming or find yourself drowning in other people's details.

IT'S OKAY TO say no.

I used to say yes—a lot. I said yes so much that my work-load grew to epic proportions. I felt stressed out. I felt pulled in too many directions. I felt as if I was failing everyone, especially my daughter, because there simply weren't enough hours in every day to get it all done and still, you know, sleep. I ran around in circles a lot. I did a lot of stuff for free or for publicity or for favors. Or all three. My life was a "favors for free publicity" free-for-all!

When you make it up every day, sometimes you forget that you are the one making it up. If you aren't going to take control of your time, your days, your focus, there will be an endless stream of folks willing to take control for you. It's a female thing to want to help, please, appease, illuminate, enlighten, and entertain. Or maybe it's just a thing some folks do because they want to "do the right thing." Whatever that is, I did a lot of it. Sure, I will review your book! Sure, I will share your link! Sure, I will review your product! Sure, I will respond to that phone call, email, text, FB message, tweet!

I said yes and yes and yes until my work and my life began to spin out of control. I was running out of time for lounging around in silk pajamas and drinking vodka. I was freaking out about things I "had to do" that were basically favors. I wasn't getting the important stuff done because too much of my time was being spent on a vast array of things that did not actually need to be done. I had to reevaluate to find balance.

I learned a lot from this.

IF YOU WANT to successfully work for yourself, you have to focus relentlessly on your goals.

You can pay it forward, sideways, and backward as long as you don't let the paying of it take up so much of your time that you have no more time to make the magic happen. The thing is, whether you work for yourself or for someone else, you have to spend most of your work time working. Then a small portion of your time can be devoted to what I call "things I said yes to," which is grammatically incorrect but vernacularly acceptable. "Vernacularly" is not a word. I digress. What was I discussing? Oh yes, things I said yes to. You can only say yes to so much and then you have to stop saying yes, unless it is a true emergency or a truly important cause.

I made a folder, a virtual folder. I called it my "things I said yes to" folder. The more we say yes, the more beholden we are to these little agreements that seem innocuous enough until they begin multiplying exponentially while gathering in a folder in our email. When mine was virtually full, I started saying no.

I also reminded myself, regardless of increasingly aggressive follow-up emails, that I did not owe perfect strangers or even imperfect acquaintances replies to every random request. The DELETE button became my friend. I stopped showing my panties to everyone who asked. I started making better use of my time. I got productive! Did I make some people sad? Probably, and for that I am sorry. I don't wish to make people sad. I don't wish to hurt people's feelings. I just have to focus my energy on making the magic every day, and sometimes I share what I've learned here or on my social media platforms, which is my small way of giving back.

It's okay to say no. It's all about balance. You can't be everything to everyone or even most things to most everyone. You can only do what you can do, be kind and loving without giving it all away, and hope that, in the final analysis, you did your best and that was enough. It is not your job to make other people happy. It is other people's job to make themselves happy. It is your job to make yourself happy. And we all know that when Mama is happy, everyone is happy.

That's something we can all say yes to.

FIVE

flummoxed

WHO'S THAT
WOMAN IN THE
MIRROR AND
WHAT HAS SHE
DONE WITH ME?

AGING IN A HI-DEF REALITY

When I began appearing as a guest expert on a home shopping network, they switched to hi-def cameras and the panic bells went off. Every wrinkle, every pore, even the tiniest little flaws were exponentially exaggerated. None of the old makeup tricks worked anymore. Faux tans looked horrid. Anyone over the age of 25 looked old. As a video editor once said to me while we reviewed my footage on a large screen, "Hi-def is a cruel, cruel mistress." Wince. Because working on camera was a job I enjoyed and wished to keep, I opted for Botox and fillers. They work well when used judiciously. Add a little too much and you start to look frozen, pulled, and poufed, as if your face were straining to escape its skin. Enter airbrush makeup and softer lighting, and we all exhaled. We were, as best as we could, navigating the complexities of aging in a hi-def reality, although it was a serious shock to see yourself in the monitor in close-up and wonder, "Wow, is that really what I look like?"

The answer is, yes . . . and no. It's really what you look like if you're being examined under a microscope, but the truth is, in real life, those tiny flaws are mostly imperceptible. We see them, but, for the most part, others don't. And the flaws, wrinkles, and freckles make us who we are; they are the sum total of our experiences. There is something to be said for embracing them, though, honestly, that won't get you far on TV.

Photo retouching techniques in the digital age have progressed to the point where most of what we see in print and on the web is so heavily retouched it's no longer a representation of reality. We live in an age of selfies and photobombs, Facebook, and Instagram, Botox and fillers, thigh gaps and spackle. We are looking at ourselves more intently, holding a hi-def camera at arm's length and shooting endless photos of ourselves. We are seeing our faces too much, too closely, and with far too much detail. In contrast, we are bombarded with images of women who have been lasered, filled, lifted, and airbrushed into almost cartoon representations of their former selves. Add to that the refusal of most of the celebrities to admit the amount of work they've had done and it's easy to see why beauty and skin care comprise a multibillion-dollar industry. So many of us are seeking that elusive fountain of youth and miracle in a bottle or syringe. We ask ourselves, "If she looks that good, why do I look so bad?" It's hard for the average Jane to feel good about her aging face when celebrity women over 50 and even in their 60s and 70s seem frozen in time.

Post-Grammys, I once stumbled onto a thread on social media started by a former silver screen siren of a certain age. She'd posted a link to an article with a very unflattering photo of Madonna, who had been recently Botoxed and freshly filled. The comments were illuminating and disturbing. People were attacking her, on the one hand, for having too much work done, and on the other for looking too old. I liked the suit and thought she looked great. She was 55, after all, not

30. Plus, in a sea of boring, frothy, safe choices, she stood out as a risk taker. Most of the attacks were coming from men, which I found fascinating. No one was harping on how old Steven Tyler, Dave Grohl, or Sir Paul McCartney look. Unfair, but not shocking.

It seems to me that Madonna should do exactly as she pleases, and I think that's true of all women. I don't quite know how one ages gracefully in a hi-def world, especially if one is a celebrity. It's all complicated by technology. I don't have the answers. I fully understand wanting to hold on to beauty a little longer. I am personally fighting these demons, trying to find balance, and opening myself up to accepting some of the inevitable changes that aging brings while feeling okay about wanting to change the things I can't accept. We all get old, if we're lucky. I am also fully aware of how much work and how much photo editing is done in the media, and how unrealistic it all is. I can look at the on-screen face of a celebrity who insists she's had no work done at all and tell you precisely what she's had done. It's her job, after all, to look good on camera, and a little nip here and tuck there fall within her job requirements, at least in our current climate.

I do wonder, though, why the pressure is so much more intense on women than on men. Why do we pick apart female celebrities who are damned if they do and damned if they don't, and let the men slide? Why can't we allow all of us to choose what makes us happy? I get what the pressures of the hi-def age are. I know that putting yourself in the spotlight means subjecting yourself to public scrutiny. I just don't get why we can't give each other and ourselves a little breathing room.

BREATHING ROOM

We get very comfortable carrying baggage that no longer serves us, and which is packed with half-truths and lies. That baggage, stuffed with the ugly and the unwanted, gets dragged around year after year. Eventually, we come to feel as if it is a part of us. We forget that we picked it up on the journey, that we pack our bags, and that we can unpack them, dump the contents, and leave them behind. I am unpacking like a madwoman and dumping out a lifetime of crap.

Talk about a de-stash!

I have been thinking deeply about aging, women, beauty, fashion, self-image, the media, and the messages we send to young women. I've had some complicated conversations with other women of a certain age over the past few years. Many of them believe that women who dye their hair, wear makeup, or opt for plastic surgery are not authentic and therefore are making it harder for "the rest of us" to age gracefully. I find these thoughts troubling. Cynicism, insecurity, and rage bubble quietly underneath these thoughts. On the one hand, I agree that the media sets impossible beauty standards. I also agree that when women lie about having work done, it makes it harder for the rest of us. With the advent of new technology, we can literally transform someone through pixels, poisons, and fillers to a level of physical perfection that is impossible to achieve. How can real women compete with surgically and digitally enhanced illusions?

But there is the rub, Why must we compete at all?

Why do we get angry when other women choose not to embrace their wrinkles, gray hair, sagging chin, or physical "imperfections"? Does it really matter? Why are we so certain that our way of moving through the world is the only way that has merit? Wrinkles may be beautiful to you, but not so much to someone else. So what? Isn't the message that women must age gracefully and fade into the background just as rigid and unyielding as the one that tells women they need to stay young, powdered, and pretty?

I am not afraid or ashamed to admit that I like makeup. I dye my hair. I get excited about a new pair of shoes. I have had a syringe or two of Botox in my brow. I suppose I may be judged shallow and vain, but I don't define myself by my exterior. These are things I do for me, not for the rest of the world. I get to decide what makes me happy when I get up and look in the mirror. I don't delude myself into thinking that my looks are all that I have to offer. What I have to offer is infinitely more rich and soulful than my appearance. What I have to offer is not something you can find in a mirror, a bottle, or a syringe. The message I choose to send to the young woman I raised is that a woman gets to choose how she festoons herself and that it is okay for her to choose what makes her happy.

In the final analysis, we are not defined by our exterior, but by our character. We can wrap ourselves up however we like, with wrinkles or not, rouged or au naturel, but it's all just wrapping. If we truly want to shift the dialogue and the zeitgeist, these are the questions we should be asking: How do you move through the world? What do you value in yourself and others? What do you have to offer to the conversation? What gets you excited to jump out of bed every morning and hit the ground running? How do you treat other people?

We can't get to those questions when we're too busy dismissing each other on the basis of our appearance.

You are no more special or exceptional because you choose to embrace gravity than you are if you choose to defy it. Life is too short to take any of it too seriously. Every woman should do what makes her happy. Regardless of how we feel about it, the rest of us gals should mind our own damn business. We define ourselves, the world does not define us. If you choose to be offended or angry because of how another woman chooses to look, that's something for you to explore. What is the source of your anger? In what way do the choices other women make about how they present themselves affect you? Perhaps you're projecting your own insecurities about aging on her. If so, maybe it's time to make peace with getting older and make room for other women to age in the manner they please. I bet you'll feel a lot happier if you do.

NO CHISKERS FOR OLD WOMEN

I have asked my family for one small favor. No matter how old I am, how infirm I might become, or how little I recall, please, for the love of all things holy, do not let my chiskers grow into long chin hairs. Grab the tweezers and pluck those fuckers. Pluck every last one of them. Even if they show up overnight in clusters of 10, banish them from my face. I cannot stand the thought of lying there in a hideous hospital gown, coif askew, with a thin dribble of drool dripping from the corners of my mouth into a mini-forest of chin hairs. I hate them with a passion that is almost as intense as my hatred of mayonnaise and cellulite. If you wish to grow your chiskers long, braid them, bead them, display them proudly—that's none of my damn business. I intend to remain chisker-free until the bitter end. No chiskers for this old woman. Not now, not ever.

PLUCK IT, I'M 50!

Hello, Gorgeous!

. . . is what I say to my reflection in the mirror every morning. Is that so wrong?

There is a fair amount of squinting that precedes this proclamation. I am somewhat ashamed to admit this, because, for fuck's sake, I'm a grown-ass woman and I need to learn to let go of the need to feel pretty. Also, I look damn good, even without squinting, from the right angle, with the proper lighting, and after a good night's rest and a sufficient amount of moisturizer, unless I shove a magnifying mirror at my face, then all bets are off.

My daughter took our magnifying mirror with her to college and I've been using a little 10x compact mirror since. A magnifying mirror helps with things like applying liquid liner, attaching false eyelashes, filling in eyebrows, or plucking random hairs. I need to remove my glasses to perform these tasks, and without them—and magnification—I can't see for shit. One of the cool things about being over 50 is that random hairs sprout overnight in all manner of strange places. Then we play the game I call find that random hair! Even more fun, random hairs seem to enjoy sprouting in groups. So, it's more like, find those random hairs! Huzzah!

I have a very good pair of tweezers. They were a considered purchase. After several years of deliberation and frustration with a mediocre pair of tweezers, I took the plunge. Fair warning, good tweezers are sharp, so a magnifying mirror is important to avoid plucking your skin with the hairs. Trust me when I tell you, this is painful.

This leads me to yesterday, when I decided it was high time I replaced my errant magnifying mirror. I perused a panoply of choices in the beauty aisle at a big-box retailer. I settled on a swiveling silver model. Then I spied, with my little eye, the number and letter combo 12x on a sticker emblazoned on a smaller mirror.

12x?! What? They make such a thing?

Dare I pick this 12x magnifying mirror up and look into it? I dared.

This was followed by a horrified gasp as I realized the proliferation of random hairs was far worse than my 10x mirror had led me to believe. Damn you, 10x mirror! How could you let me wander around with a plethora of whiskers jutting defiantly from my crater-sized pores? What the hell is wrong with you?

Mirror, mirror, on the wall, who's the biggest lying liar of them all?

You are, bitch.

We're finished. Kindly pack up your belongings and get out. You've been replaced by my new best frenemy, 12x mirror. This morning, I spent the better part of ten minutes canoodling with my new frenemy, tweezers in hand. I'm pleased to report that a shocking number of previously elusive random hairs met their untimely demise.

This is my life, now. I have come to accept it. The hair thing is not going to improve. In the grand cosmic scheme, the indignities of aging most definitely beat the alternative. Still, it makes me feel better to battle back the ravages of time even if I can't keep them from advancing. I don't like random hairs and I'll be damned if I will let them win.

Pluck it, I'm 50.

OLD, FAT, AND OVER IT

For the past few years, I've been occasionally referring to myself as old and fat. I was joking, but not really. It was a defense mechanism. The truth is, I felt old and fat, so I deflected my unhappiness about my age and weight with vaguely witty, self-effacing comments. It wasn't funny and it wasn't sending a good message to my daughter.

> **YOU BECOME WHAT** you think. Your words
> have power. *Old* and *fat*—they're just
> words. But words can be weapons.

Sometimes the deepest wounds are the ones we inflict on ourselves. As we age, in a world that demands that women be young, pretty, and thin, it's not surprising that women over 50 and over size 8 feel old, fat, and unattractive. Even in the older fashion blogger community, the popular ladies are super-model thin and pretty. It is fashion, after all, and fashion prefers the young, thin, and pretty.

I was talking with my hairdresser recently and she was bemoaning the fact that the men who run the hair color company she works with insist on only featuring young, slender models in their advertising and hair shows. She's asked repeatedly to feature a wider variety of women, especially since a majority of women who color their hair are older. They've balked at her request. Do you hear a recurring theme? Men seem compelled to tell women what they want.

A multibillion-dollar industry is built on and fueled by our insecurities as women. It's a vicious cycle, designed to erode our self-confidence and dig into our bank accounts. That industry tells us from a very young age that we are not good enough and we will not be good enough unless we wear their jeans, hide our faces behind their makeup, starve our bodies into submission under their diet plan, or slather ourselves with their skin creams. Our collective unconsciousness is built around the mythology that being young, thin, and pretty is the key to happiness. That's a powerful myth.

I was young, thin, and pretty for years, and you know what? I wasn't happy. I felt unworthy. I still wasn't good enough, according to that mythology. My breasts were too small, my bottom too curvy, my skin was too pale, my hair too unruly. I look back now at photos of that girl and I am sad for her. I am sad for that smart, funny, talented, beautiful girl who felt she wasn't good enough. She was good enough. I am good enough. Her value then and my value now have nothing to do with appearances. In the grand cosmic scheme, my age and weight are irrelevant to the totality of who I am and what I have to offer to the world. Those numbers only have the power that I give them. Those numbers, and the messages sent by giving them power, deflect attention from my real value.

I have had enough of the lie that I'm not good enough. I reject the idea that happiness can be found in a jar or a lipstick case or a new pair of jeans. I am worthy, I am beautiful, I am limitless. And you know what, my dear? So are you.

THEM'S THE LUMPS

A (NOT) LOVE SONG FOR CELLULITE

Though the sum of my parts is appealing,
Some of my parts send me reeling.
Can I love me enough, while not loving this stuff?
Lumps do not summon any fond feeling.

I find curves, for the record, delightful,
They're bodacious, beguiling, not frightful.
"Lumps are curves!" some might say. I say "Send them away!"
I'm convinced their intention is spiteful.

"It's all part of the journey, so face it.
Just accept that you cannot erase it!"
Dimples, ripples, bumps, saggy bits, and funky bumps,
Cellulite? I refuse to embrace it.

Some real women have curves, some real women do not have curves, and some real women have lumps. I currently have curves, I used to lack curves, but I have always had lumps. My lumps, which started on my butt way back when I entered puberty, have made their way toward my ankles and up toward my neck. They've crept all over me like poison ivy, showing up here, there, and everywhere without notice or invitation. How rude.

I have lumps on my thighs, lumps on my calves, and lumps on my stomach. I have lumps on my back, and lumps on my kneecaps.

Of all the lumps that I despise, and I despise them all, none elicits more distaste than the lumps on my upper arms. Bastards. I call this phenomenon *armulite*, an elision of *arm* and *cellulite*. I don't mind curves, but for fuck's sake what is up with the lumps?

Maybe one day I shall overcome my distaste for lumps. Probably not, but I strive.

Because I despise lumps, I cover them as much as possible. I don't wear shorts. I don't wear short skirts. I wear tights or leggings when I wear dresses. I wear sweaters in the middle of August. I wear cover-ups at the beach. I would not wear a bathing suit in public if you paid me. Well, it depends on how much. If we're talking five figures, then perhaps I could be persuaded. Let's talk. But I digress. I categorically refuse to show my upper arms in public unless there is a significant amount of money involved. This is irrational. It is absurd. It is self-defeating, especially since I'm experiencing my own personal summer 365 days a year. I hate being hot, but I hate lumps more.

Lumps trump heat.

As much as I hate lumps, I showed my upper arms to fitness guru Harley Pasternak on national TV recently. I removed my jacket, wiggled my saggy arm fat, and pointed out the armulite. This flies in the face of everything I've written here, I know. I thought if I showed my lumps, perhaps other lumpy women would feel a little less awful about theirs. Joan of Arc has nothing on me, baby. Harley gave me some great suggestions for exercising the lumps away, but argh—exercise? I am exhausted just thinking about it. Who has the time? I'm far too busy shopping for all-season sweaters and patterned leggings.

DEAR NECK

Nora Ephron isn't the only woman over 50 who feels bad about her neck. We all do, honey. Unless you can afford a trip to the plastic surgeon, your neck is going to give you away like Benedict Arnold.

Dear Neck,

Hello, old friend. We've been together for 55 years now, which is almost impossible to believe. Let me begin by assuring you that I adore you, always have. You've been the perfect accompaniment to the revolving array of necklaces, scarves, collars, and other adornments I've strewn upon you over the years. I could not have asked for a better neck unless I was Audrey Hepburn. Thank you, from the bottom of my jawbone to the top of my collarbone, thank you.

The thing is, though, lately you've changed. Quite frankly, I'm not loving the new you. It started with a few creases, nothing I couldn't overlook, but then the sagging began. It's progressed with alarming rapidity. I catch it randomly in my reflection when the light is just right, or, more aptly, just wrong. "No, no, no, no, what is that?!" It's really, really making me sad.

Ugh, this is hard.

I have tried slathering you with rich creams saturated with a heady combination of empty promises and the stem cells of rare exotic plants. I have ardently practiced an increasingly complex regimen of daily neck yoga. I have soothed you with sweet words and begged you to reconsider, yet you defy my every protestation with a relentless downward march. It's really gotten out of control, neck, and it needs to stop.

It seems we have reached an impasse that even a drawer filled with turtleneck dickies cannot solve. I'm afraid I will be forced to accept your refusal to retreat until I am able to cobble together enough funds to combat further assault. Until then, I ask only that your descent be slowed by my heartfelt vociferous protestations. And while I'm here, please inform your friends, the jowls, that they're also on notice.

Love,
Margot

YOU LOOK GOOD, FOR YOUR AGE

"You're how old? Wow! You look good for your age!"

This one—this one is really insidious. It's the ultimate backhanded compliment for the older woman. Yet, it's generally received with giddy enthusiasm, "I do? Thank GOD!"

Holding back the ravages of time is important in a society where women over 50 are treated like pariahs. We can't find work. We can't find clothes. We can't find our faces represented in traditional media. Unless we find a way to maintain a semblance of perpetual youth, we are shown the virtual door. Please make room for a younger model. Thank you. Are you still here? Disappear already, will you?

Let's parse the "You look good for your age" compliment, shall we? It's tricky because, on the one hand, it clearly states that "you look good." That's a positive, right? We all want to look good because we live in a world that is mostly driven by appearances. Looking bad won't get you any prizes. On the other hand, can we embrace the "you look good" portion of the equation while rejecting the second half? What exactly does "for your age" mean? Does it mean that you look 5 years younger, 10 years younger, 15 percent less saggy, 25 percent less wrinkly? If you looked like this, but you were 5 or 10 years younger, would you then look bad for your age? Is there a chart somewhere we might reference?

Why are we so terrified of aging? Why aren't we embracing the wisdom, the power, the beauty, the wonder of being alive this long and having survived this much?

Gravity, collagen depletion, and sun damage conspire to change our faces, and, as time progresses, turn us into strangers to ourselves. "Where'd that fabulous girl go and who the hell is this?," we ask as we gaze at that old woman in the mirror. Once she's old, who's there to tell her that she looks good?

Then the media trots out the same collection of ageless beauties, who have the luxury of great bones and great plastic surgeons, and say, "Look at her, she looks AMAZING for her age." As if to say, "Hey, old bag over there, what's your excuse?" Because looking good at every age is far more important for a woman than being wise, or accomplished, or compassionate, right?

There is a definite beauty to a woman whose aging face no longer reflects impossible societal standards or the need to attract the male gaze. Our face reflects our unique life experience, the journey we take from youth to maturity. Every wrinkle, every shift in the terrain tells a story of a life lived, of adventures and heartbreaks, and triumphs and tragedies. That's real beauty.

I am trying to navigate the shift as I age, trying to find a way to embrace the changes, instead of fearing them. I like a compliment as much as the next gal, but I want to love myself enough to let go of the need for that kind of external affirmation. My face is a canvas and life is the artist.

That's something resonant.

That's something magical.

That's alchemy.

FLABBY
EARLESS
RAZZLED
ORLORN
LUMMOXED
FLEXIBLE
LAMBOYANT
ASHIONABLE
FEMINIST
FREE

SIX

flamboyant

A GIRL'S GUIDE TO CANDY-COLORED HAIR, BOTOX, AND HOPE IN A JAR

WHAT I LEARNED FROM HAVING PINK HAIR

I've been dyeing my hair since I was in my 20s. The only break I took was while I was pregnant in my mid-30s. Once I hit my mid-40s, I decided to go blonde. I love gray hair on other women, and I'm a believer in each of us doing what works for us. Gray just wasn't going to work for my pale skin or my overall happacity. Two years ago, I went pink.

It's funny how changing your hair color can change your life. Over the past 55 years, I have rocked virtually every color known to hair, a plethora of colors that go far beyond the natural spectrum. Black, platinum, soft-golden blonde, every shade of red from copper to magenta, blue, baby-poop green (a most unfortunate accident), orange, yellow, brown, gray . . . and finally the one color after which I have lusted since I first picked up a box of Miss Clairol oh so many moons ago. My natural hair is a most delightful shade of reddish brown, naturally imbued with streaks of blonde and red. Over the past so many years, though, it has become saltier and less pepper-y.

I had a stash of candy-colored wigs that I used to wear to special events, but they met an untimely demise after a particularly humid summer in the Smoky Mountains. While preparing to move, I discovered they'd been decimated by mold. Sad face, goodbye candy-colored wigs.

When my hairstylist showed me a bold new hair color line, it was clear that cosmetology had progressed enough to allow me to have the long-desired, candy-colored tresses without destroying my hair. No bleaching to platinum, we could achieve pink, lifting the base color to the same blonde I'd been sporting for the past seven years. Good grief, when did I fall into such a hair color rut?! On a whim, after I decided that at my age I had earned the right to return to my more off-colored, past hair dye experiments, I decided to go for it!

"PINK ME!" I declared.

So began a most fascinating journey into the complexities of human nature. Twelve years of waiting tables and 55 years of studied observation have confirmed that people, for the most part, are all seeking the same things. We want to be loved. We long to be cherished. We ache for connection. We desire, above all things, to be accepted exactly as we are. Yet, we find it almost impossible to offer these things to others. The cycle of being hurt, feeling left out, finding ourselves disconnected because of an offhanded comment or worse, a calculated attack, breeds more of the same. We protect ourselves from pain, but in the process, we miss out on opportunities for joy.

Those who dare to live out loud, defy the rules, and embrace what makes them different serve as a mirror for those who are afraid to do the same.

"Hey! Put that away! Be quiet, calm down, blend in!" the world shouts.

Eventually we choose to comply or we say, "To hell with that!"

THE FUNNY THING is, when we let go of being who we think the world wants us to be, we find ourselves being met with the acceptance that eluded us in the years we spent pretending to be someone else.

It took dyeing my hair pink to free myself from the need to fit in, and I learned so much in the process.

Pink hair makes most people happy.

Yup. People smile at me wherever I go. I get so many compliments. They are curious, in a good way. Pink hair is a conversation starter and a goodwill harbinger. I've always been a friendly person, but now I'm finding a greater level of reciprocation. Pink is a pretty, happy, hopeful color, and it really resonates with a lot of folks. How cool is that?

Kids think pink hair is magical.

It's the most miraculous, wonderful thing! Kids gasp, smile, squeal when they see pink hair. "MOM! She has PINK HAIR!" they say. The moms then apologize, but I say, "Oh it's fine. I love kids!" I have stood in the aisles at craft stores and beauty chains dispensing advice on how to temporarily add pink to a child's hair without damaging it. Honestly, I think kids are right: Pink hair is magic. Last year a little girl shyly approached our dinner table holding her stuffed rabbit closely and whispered, "Excuse me. I just wanted to say that your hair is beautiful." I almost fell off my chair. As we were leaving, I gave her my pink floral pin, and she was so excited. We both won that day. Now that really is magical.

Some pink-haired ladies have a stick up their butts.

Sorry, hate to report this, but alas it is true. I was shocked at the mean girl antics of a few pink-coiffed adult women. They forgot that pink hair is a choice anyone can make and if it weren't, there wouldn't be a plethora of hair dyes in varying shades of pink on the market. They felt that pink hair made them special and that if other women had pink hair, it threatened their specialness. Silly ladies. What makes us special has absolutely nothing to do with our hair. The more candy-colored-haired ladies, the more fabulous the party! Bring it on! I love seeing my feeds filling up with ladies who have taken the plunge. As for the mean girls, get over yourselves. No one is copying you. You did not invent pink hair, rockabilly dresses, glitter, polka dots, decoupage, or liquid eyeliner, and neither did I. Live and let live, gals. Life is too short for that shit.

Most pink-haired ladies really get it.

Most of the time, I've had wonderful experiences meeting and talking with pink-haired (or candy-color-haired) ladies. It takes a certain kind of fearlessness to be willing to sport candy-colored hair. When we see each other, we smile that knowing smile that says, "Yup, me too. Rock on!" Sometimes we share hair dye secrets. Sometimes we high-five. Sometimes it opens a door to much deeper and more lively conversations. It's like we're part of a secret society of women who really don't give a flying fuck what society thinks of us. I love that. That's the stuff right there. More of this and less of the other, please, and thank you.

Pink hair requires time and monetary commitment.

In order for me to maintain this mane, it requires a fair amount of effort. I have to add color to my conditioner and apply it with gloves when I wash my tresses. It takes four hours at the salon to properly color this hair so it looks even and vibrant. My gray roots show much faster, which was problematic until a matching powder was created to apply in between color appointments. I have to wear hats when I'm frolicking in the sun. I can't swim in a pool or the ocean or anywhere without a bathing cap. If I get caught in a rainstorm without an umbrella, I look like Carrie. Even working with a pro, we're still learning how to make it work.

Be prepared to change your wardrobe if you dye your hair pink.

Alas, many of my formerly favorite outfits look dreadful when paired with pink hair. As a design expert who is relentlessly specific about color, I simply can't go around clashing. I find black, white, chartreuse, orange, yellow, navy blue, gray, and kelly green work very well for me. You can do a tonal thing with shades of pink as well. Depending on the tone and intensity of your pink and the color of your skin, you may find a different palette suits you.

You cannot hide with pink hair.

If you're shy and retiring or currently on the lam, it may not be the best plan to go pink. People can find you in a crowd in a heartbeat. You will be known, hereafter, as the "lady (or gentleman) with the pink hair." On the other hand, if you've been feeling invisible, going pink will most definitely change that. People comment on my hair constantly, and I'm okay with that.

Pink hair helps give other people permission to color outside of the lines.

No, it's true! I have had so many older women stop and compliment me and then say, "I wish I could do that. It's so beautiful!" To which I reply, "But you can!" Then they say, "But what will the gals think?!" To which I reply, "They'll think you're brave and brilliant." Several folks I know have decided to take the plunge and go pink, or blue, or green! I love that!

Dyeing my hair pink is one of the best things I have ever done. It helped me free myself from any final vestiges of desire to make myself less Technicolor. It's made even the most humdrum days exciting. I wish I had done it years ago. I have no plans to go back.

DYE YOUR HAIR pink, let it go glorious gray, shave it off, grow it down to the floor. It's just hair, after all.

WOMEN, HAIR, AND POWER

Once a year I throw caution to the wind and enjoy a Shamrock Shake from McDonalds®. This delicious, neon-green concoction is my annual guilty pleasure. No lectures, please. I'm old enough to make my own gastronomic decisions.

So it was that last week I found myself sitting in the passenger seat at the drive-through of McDonalds, as the cashier yelled over to me, "How did you get your husband to let you do that to your hair?"

Wait, what? Did this 20-something woman just insinuate that I need permission from a man to make decisions about my appearance?

"Because I'm an adult," I replied, "I don't need permission to dye my hair pink."

"My husband won't let me dye my hair pink. Black, red, blonde, he even says I can dye it green . . . but not pink." She looked at me with a combination of longing, confusion, and amazement. How did I achieve the impossible? How could I do something so utterly defiant of my husband's right to demand that I follow his rules?

How indeed.

"Do what makes you happy and tell him to get over it," I said, smiling.

She demurred, then replied, "Oh, he'd never let me do that."

I had no answer. What can you say to a woman who has ceded her power to someone else? She's telling herself this story and for her it's true.

And with that I paid for my shake and drove off into the sunset.

I'm still disturbed by this exchange. Are young women really this afraid, still, of being true to their desires? Do women still need permission to do what makes them happy? Have we progressed at all?

The truth is, there is a lot of stuff wrapped up in our hair. Figuratively speaking, and sometimes literally. My husband prefers my hair worn long—he didn't think he'd like pink hair, but he does. I don't style my hair for him, I style my hair for me. If I wanted to shave my head and tattoo my scalp like an 8 ball, he'd deal with it. He's grown rather accustomed to my independence. In the many years that we've been together I have cut my hair off, grown it long, cut it off again, dyed it white, black, red, blonde, brown, and pink. He might not always it, and he'll let me know his feelings, as he is nothing if not straightforward and painfully blunt. We've approached our marriage as a partnership, not a benevolent (or malevolent) dictatorship. He knew going into this arrangement that I was a woman with a mind and a scalp of her own.

Being a person who has spent a lifetime dealing with unruly, ill-mannered, supersized, frizz-prone, and increasingly confounding locks, I have never been in love with my hair. I have never felt even the slightest fealty to preserving my hair precisely as it grows from my scalp. There's something deliciously liberating about doing whatever the hell you fancy with your hair, knowing that it will grow back defying whatever adjustments you've made. Oh yeah, horrid hair, well here's one for you. Take that!

You see, there's a thread here around women, power, and hair, and it's a fascinating one.

It's a thread tied up in freedom or unraveled by the lack thereof. It's about power. It's about magic. It's about conformity and adherence to rules. It's a thread that confounds and confronts. We can be bound by it or we can allow it to set us free. The choice is ours, regardless of what tales we choose to tell ourselves. You do not need permission to choose joy, whatever that means to you. If you do, it may be time to reevaluate your reality.

MY HAIR-STORY

If you take a moment to gaze at the photo above, you will note my picture. It's hard to miss, really, as it's absurdly large. Once you got over the size of my giant head staring back at you, you might think, wow, she's got pretty hair.

You would be wrong.

Yes, I have fooled you and everyone except those who know me best into believing that I was blessed with hair that would make Marcia Brady swoon. But I was not blessed in the hair department. Actually, I have plenty of hair, enough for approximately three people. The hair fairy triply blessed me, which may explain why the boob fairy got bored and wandered off elsewhere. Damn you, hair fairy. I have epic amounts of hair. Wild, crazy, frizzy, wavy, funky, defiant hair (much like the person upon whom it grows). In the never-ending attempt to wrangle this wild hair, I have had some dreadful hairstyles. Tragic. Epic. Hideous. "What the French toast?" hairstyles. It's hard to believe that one child could possibly have taken so many horrid school photos. Yet, somehow, I did.

Kookie, Kookie, lend me your comb!

Or your brush!

Or a weed-whacker.

Whatever.

We begin with what is best described as a disheveled ball of strawberry blonde/light brown-ish, wispy cotton candy fluff that grew out from center in all directions. The only course of action was securing it back with ponytail holders (or hair bows if you live in East Tennessee, but we lived in eastern Pennsylvania, so . . .). As you can see in this series, which I'm calling The Early Years, my mother did her best to tame the beast. Unfortunately, the beast won the battle.

These are the two best hair days I had in those early years. This slicked-back look is achieved with a comb, water, and a lot of patience. I call the one on the right "cork screwed." Remember those ponytail holders with the plastic balls? Do they still make those? Because if they do, I would totally rock them!

After endless admonishments from perfectly dreadful strangers, who felt it was their duty to tell my mother to brush my hair, she gave up. My hair would not bend to the brush, the comb, or the siren call of Dippity Do®. In fact, it Dippity Didn't. In exasperation, my mother cut it all off, and voilà! How fetching is this? Is she a girl? Is she a boy? Did she have head lice? Well, at least she has nice eyes!

But wait, check out this baffling progression from dreadful pixie into some sort of shag cut gone terribly wrong. What are these tendrils and why? Did they sprout overnight like weeds? Paging Florence Henderson! Someone help this poor child! You will note that, along with my hair, my teeth decided to join the party and grow in opposite directions. Check out that canine on the right. Now that's a tooth! (I am digging the Cheshire cat Izod Lacoste knockoff, though.)

From there, the hair grew and grew and grew and grew some more. As you can see, around sixth grade, I reverted to the ponytail holder solution.

Ah, the center part, I knew you well. You were not my friend, center part.

Remember Dorothy Hamill? I do! This is my attempt to smoosh my hair into a Dorothy-inspired wedge cut. Fetching, no? I won the Public Speaking Contest that year, along with a host of other awards. Shockingly, I did not win the Best Hair Award.

Braces were applied to my teeth, forcing them into submission. Then came the perm rods to force my hair into submission! Hooray! I showed that hair. Whodunit? I don't remember, but they really should have refrained. Shirt, 1, Perm, 0.

Ah, that's a little better! Braces off and teeth managed! Thank the good lord for Farrah, who helped transition me into layers, and Olivia Newton-John, who introduced me to the joyous wonders of the headband.

Post-Farrah/Olivia, I channeled Joan Jett, finding solace in the shag. Don't ask about the eye shadow. No, really. Don't ask.

Then came the Punk Rock Years and the gleeful discoveries of baby bangs, bleach, jet-black hair dye, and Aqua Net® Extra Super Hold. Heady days, indeed. Pardon the pun. You may be interested to know that I was in a band called Big Hair. You can't make this stuff up, people.

Next came blonde hair, red hair, crazy hair.

Finally, we arrive at keratin-tamed pink hair.

Sisters of the Wild Hair—and I know you're out there—take comfort in the knowledge that you are not alone. I feel your pain, truly.

ARCHITECTURAL PRESERVATION

I think it's high time someone pointed out that the empress has no clothes. The cult of beauty apparently requires an unspoken agreement to *never* admit that we do anything to "enhance" our features. It means women who have spent tens of thousands of dollars on what I like to call "architectural preservation" refuse to divulge that they've done anything, let alone what they've done, when, and how often.

It's amazing how many women in the public eye are so well preserved after 40, isn't it? I mean, they all swear they don't use Botox, have fillers, wear false eyelashes or falsies, have boob jobs or nose jobs or tummy tucks or fanny lifts or chin implants or butt injections or face-lifts. They are, apparently, every last one of them (with the exception of the DIVINELY frank Joan Rivers), natural beauties who never age.

What is the reason for the deluge of denial? To pretend you never age when you're stacking the deck makes women who can't afford or don't wish to have cosmetic surgery wonder if there is something wrong with them. Most of these celebrities are rail-thin; even if they were still young they'd have parenthetical lines around their mouths, yet amazingly they do not.

It's magic!

Or they've all got a painting hidden in a closet or they bathe in the blood of ritually sacrificed chipmunks on the full moon every month.

They've ALL had some work done. It's part of the deal. It's like getting a tune-up on your car or replacing your engine after 100,000 miles. It's what they need to do to keep getting work. That's the hard, cold truth of it. If they had knee surgery so they could still play football, we wouldn't bat a single eye-lash. What's the difference, really? Why do they all lie about it? Do they honestly think we all believe that none of them have had work done? That their lips puffed up overnight, their nose shrank, their jowls took a trip to Tahiti, and their foreheads are naturally as smooth as a baby's bottom?

Let me be clear: I think it's entirely up to you to age grace-fully, to age disgracefully, or to fight it tooth and nail. That choice is yours and yours alone. I think every gal should do what makes her happy. But I *don't* think gals should lie about doing it, because that just adds to the never-ending pressure on women to be perfect.

There's absolutely nothing wrong with a little architectural preservation, but there is something wrong with living a lie.

ZEN IN A SYRINGE

I used to get Botox on a regular basis. Yes, it's a deadly poison, but it's fabulous! I call it Zen in a syringe. Not only does it make your wrinkles go away, it freezes the muscles that make the wrin-kles. The muscles in your forehead and between your eyes are the ones you use to make angry faces. Flex those muscles right now. Do you feel that? That's what angry feels like. Okay, stop feeling that. No one likes being angry. The inability to make angry faces and therefore feel less angry is a side benefit of using Botox.

Now that I no longer get Botox, I have a permanent head-ache that lives between my eyes. I've developed a triangle-shaped wrinkle in my brow and a series of unwelcome horizontal lines on my forehead. Since my budget no longer allows for regular poison injections, I've opted for bangs.

When I used to get Botox on a regular basis, that headache disappeared. My forehead was smooth. The space between my eyes was wrinkle-free. I found myself feeling far less stressed out. In fact, I rarely got angry; the most I could muster was a slight semblance of annoyance. Meh. Then, when the Botox started wearing off, my family begged me to go get a refresher. Nobody likes Angry Mommy, least of all me.

I realize some women think that getting Botox is a mortal sin. It's gotten a bad rap after overuse by certain frozen-featured Hollywood celebrities. They have that deer-in-the-headlights look that comes from not being able to move any of the muscles in their upper face. A good plastic surgeon is an expert at using just the right amount of Botox to limit overexpression, but leave their patients with enough facial movement to appear human. No one wants to look like a Stepford Wife. I want to be careful here, though, because I try to refrain from judging other people's choices. If it makes them happy, that's their business.

A lot of women feel compelled to insist that no one use Botox.

Age gracefully, they cry!

Thanks, but no thanks, I reply!

I miss Botox. I miss not being able to make angry faces. I miss the sense of calm and rightness with the world that came from freezing my forehead muscles. I also miss being able to wear my bangs swept to the side in a sparkling barrette and not seeing wrinkles in the mirror. Oh, for those carefree, blissful, toxin-filled days!

I stopped getting Botox, due to budgetary constraints, after what I call the Year from Hell in Tennessee. This could not have been a less opportune time to cease treatment. The onslaught of menopause, the considerable stress under which I was living, and the lack of sweet poisonous tranquility proved to be a potent combination. My once-smooth forehead rapidly began producing a flurry of wrinkles.

As my mood—and forehead—continued to implode, I did some research to see if there was something to the serenity I'd previously experienced. Was it possible that not being able to make angry faces was preventing me from being angry? Was that a real thing? As it turns out, Botox fights depression. Studies have shown that not being able to make stressed-out, angry, sad faces really does make us less stressed out, angry, and sad.

It's a twofer! Sign me up.

A VISIT WITH THE BOTOX FAIRY

I have returned from my visit with the Botox Fairy. I look like a real girl now and not just a puppet on a string! Currently I look like a real duck girl, but we will all cross our fingers that my lips will return to a more normal size within the next few days. This experience was neither fun nor funny. Don't let anybody sugarcoat this one. The shots hurt. They're not in the same league as giving birth without painkillers, and I know of which I speak, but they still hurt. I currently look as though I went a few rounds with Mike Tyson and lost. It will all soften in the next few days. For your edification, education, enlightenment, and entertainment I will proceed to give you a prick-by-prick account of my journey into the world of architectural preservation.

I was given a consent form to read and fill out about Botox. I read and signed my name on the dotted line. This was with some reservations, due to the 1 percent of folks who experience a temporary eyelid droop, which would truly suck wind. I sucked it up, accepting the potential for wind sucking, and signed. I went back to a little examination room. The nurse came in and we talked about the things I wished to change and how Botox might achieve that. She took some before photos. Then she went to get the doctor. He was a very nice man with a very calm manner. I needed calm. Chatty doctors wielding needles aren't my thing.

The Botox Fairy assessed my assets and my issues. We agreed on Botox around the eyes, forehead, and in between the eyes. Then he talked to me about the three types of fillers we could use. Each one is a hyaluronic acid gel that is injected into your skin to plump up the wrinkled or recessed area. You aren't really erasing the wrinkle as much as filling it in with a viscous goop. Restylane® is the least expensive and lasts the shortest time. Juvederm® is slightly more expensive and lasts a little longer, so it's basically more bang for your buck. Radiesse® is a bit more expensive than the other two, but lasts significantly longer. Since I wasn't sure if I was going to love my new face, I opted for Juvederm. It helped that Juvederm was on a half-price special. We all know how much I love a bargain. If I love the results this time around, then I will upgrade to the longer-lasting gel. Is it just me, or does this sound like a laundry detergent comparison? Golly, I really love Juvederm, it makes my whites whiter and my colors POP!

The doctor stepped out of the room and the nurse returned and slapped some funky anesthetic goo that looked like curdled milk on my lips and marionette lines. Unfortunately, some of it made it into my mouth, so my tongue went numb and my mouth tasted yucky. The doctor returned with a little plastic case that had a lot of needles in it. Ack. They don't numb you for Botox, but the needle is very thin. It hurts. It doesn't hurt quite as much as a bee sting, but enough to make you jump and shake a little bit. Every time the needle went in there was this creepy crunching sound. It was sort of like someone eating a tortilla chip—or maybe more like a Bugle corn snack, because it's less dense—or stepping on snow that has iced up a little.

Crunch, crackle, pop.

This sound was caused by the sun damage on the surface of my skin. If you look up "white girl" in the dictionary, you'll see my photo. I do my best to avoid the sun, but I can't live in a bubble. Let me just say one word here: sunscreen. Sunscreen is your friend.

Crunch . . . crunch . . . crunch.

About six needles went into my forehead. My new bangs cover this, but I may not wish to have bangs forever. Besides, my bang-cutting skills are abysmal. Then the three or so shots that went in the lines between my eyes were followed by six more in the smile lines under my eyes.

Crunch . . . crunch . . . crunch.

It takes time for Botox to work, meaning your muscles will stop contracting, but the lines don't go away. The static or resting lines are there for good, but with continued Botox injections they will recede or soften somewhat. Whatever doesn't recede can be filled with gel. If you start using Botox sooner, then you won't get the static lines.

Botox finished. Phew . . . the creepy crunching has ceased. I bled a little bit, and I exhaled.

Onward and upward to filler land. The doctor had to numb my gums for the gel injections, so he placed a couple swabs soaked in a strong anesthetic inside my upper gums and let them sit for a moment. Then I got two big shots of painkiller there. Ouch. The second one really hurt. My mouth tasted godawful. I had to spit a few times into the sink and wipe some of the funk out of my mouth. I was totally numb, so spitting was a little tricky. Maybe "projectile drooling" would be a better description of this portion of the story. Then he began injecting the filler. I felt little to nothing—a major blessing. We did the lines with, I think, about three shots on each side, then he had to reach inside my mouth and massage the gel a little. Then we did my lips. The only part where I felt the needle was the center of the lip, but it was more of a pinch than a sting. To quote that oft-quoted film *Snow Dogs*, "More than a tickle, less than a pinch." After doing this, the doctor decided that the sides of my mouth needed a little plumping where some downturned lines had started. Since I hadn't been anesthetized here, it hurt like a mothershutyourmouth! I am glad he did it, though. It wasn't quite as painful as a piercing—a belly button piercing not an ear piercing. It hurt more than a flu shot.

That's all she wrote, and then I paid the piper and headed home. All in all, not so bad. Then you start to think, Well now there's this other thing over here. Should I fix that? The doctor asked if I wanted to erase my freckles, to which I shouted a resounding "NO! I love my freckles. Love them. They are here to stay." I must remain upright for four hours. I must not jog, dance, bounce on my trampoline, or engage in any strenuous physical activity for the next 24 to 48 hours. I think that can be arranged, unless baking five dozen of my world-famous chocolate chip-oatmeal cookies counts as strenuous physical activity. Then I am SCREWED!

My daughter says I don't look like a duck or really that different. I do look like a duck, but she's a thoughtful daughter and she knows when to lie to her mommy to spare her feelings. Just call me Duck Mom. Quack freaking quack.

There you are, folks, a play-by-play analysis of my visit to the Botox Fairy. I'll never lie about having work done.

HOPE IN A JAR

I have a drawer, as do most women of a certain age, straining at the seams with a dazzling array of lotions, potions, serums, and elixirs all promising to restore my youthful appearance. I call this the Drawer of False Promises and Shattered Dreams. When opened, it emits a heavy sigh of disappointment.

I have exfoliated, scrubbed, oxygenated, masked, massaged, soaked, slathered, poked, pinched, prodded, and prayed.

I have addressed my lack of radiance, slow cell-rate turn-over, wrinkles, fine lines, sagging, collagen depletion, age spots, inflammation, sun damage, and dreaded loss of plumpness with due reverence.

One would think that a gal who has put as many magical creams on her face and neck as I have in the endless pursuit of the fountain of youth would (in the words of Isaac Mizrahi) "look a-MAH-zing." One would be incorrect. I look good, better than some, but I do not look "a-MAH-zing." This is because, regardless of what the purveyors of these absurdly expensive snake oil concoctions in fancy jars say to get us to pony up the Benjamins, there is no lotion, potion, cream, nor serum that will restore youth.

I know this, yet every time I read an article in one of my lady magazines touting the wonders of a "game changing" new entrant into the skin care market, I am hooked. I must have this wonder cream. I know this cream is different. After all, the editors at *Marie Claire* LOVED it!

It usually goes something like this:

Squeal with delight after reading rave review of new beauty cream that is groundbreaking and revolutionary, written by a 20-something beauty editor who has nary a wrinkle on her face.

Obsess over the possibility that this beauty cream is going to change my life.

Drive to King of Prussia Mall, screaming obscenities at idiots in parking lot who seem incapable of understanding the importance of my mission.

Avoid perky salespeople wielding spray bottles of stinky perfume, stalk beauty cream like Captain Ahab after Moby Dick.

SUCCESS!

HUZZAH!

Traipse back to car with tiny striped gift bag resplendent with the first flush of new love.

Drive home, race inside, open beauty cream to chorus of angels.

Slather on face and wait. Oh yes! I feel it! Something is happening!

Continue slapping beauty cream on face twice daily for several weeks, convinced that something is indeed happening.

Face the sad truth that I have once again been flimflammed and bamboozled. Damn you, beauty cream.

Solemnly shove beauty cream into the Drawer of False Promises and Shattered Dreams.

End scene.

SEVEN

fashionable

#OVER50ANDFABULOUS

DEFINING STYLE

Many of us (including this writer) have stood in the dressing room under the horrid glow of fluorescent lights in an ill-fitting garment, mouth agape in horror.

"ACK! It looked so appealing on the mannequin!"

We've gone skipping into a shopping trip with the vague hope of feeling fabulous, only to be met by a dazzling array of unflattering fashions and unfortunate accessories. Fashion is designed for younger, thinner, mostly impossible bodies. When you're a size 2 and age 22, everything looks good on you. When you're a size 14 and age 54, it's dismal out there.

Don't give up hope. You've got this!

FUCK THE FICKLE finger of fashion. Wear
what makes you feel fantastic and do it
fearlessly. You define your style, and that's
what makes discovering it a grand adventure.

Style is a form of expression. It's an exterior manifestation of your interior world. It's a way of sharing what makes you unique through the things with which you adorn yourself. Trends come and go. Fashion is fleeting. Yet, style remains that indefinable something else. We know it when we see it, but it's hard to pin down.

Live long enough, or even live a short time with an uncanny sense of self, and you will develop a personal style. Even if it's a "non-style," it's still something that you wear every day that expresses something about you. Everyone has some kind of style, but great style is rare, and it almost always appears effortless.

Remember that Lady Godiva wore her birthday suit in public and we're still talking about her.

Now, that's defining style.

WHAT A WOMAN SHOULD NEVER WEAR:

- An air of superiority.

- A look of self-righteous indignation.

- A cloak of shame.

- Old baggage that is no longer serving her happiness.

- The marks left from a hand lifted in anger.

- The face of fear.

- Her sorrow like a millstone.

- Anything that makes her feel uncomfortable.

- Clothing specifically designed to shame her body or make her feel morally inferior.

- The weight of other people's opinions.

- The hair shirt of martyrdom.

WHAT A WOMAN
SHOULD ALWAYS WEAR:

- Her confidence.

- An air of mystery.

- A wicked grin.

- A true sense of her self-worth.

- Anything that makes her feel fabulous.

- The cape of happiness.

- Pride in her achievements.

- True joy in the success of others.

- A live-and-let-live attitude.

- A no-bullshit shield.

- A positive outlook.

- A pair of shoes that make her feel that she can kick ass, take names, and get up the next day and do it again.

- Whatever the hell she wants.

MY LIFE IN PANTIES

I'm not sure if this is yet another harbinger of aging disgracefully, but I'm admitting out loud that my panty needs have shifted dramatically over the past few years. Where I once had a drawer stuffed with lacy thongs, I now have a drawer filled with Lycra stretch hip-huggers and I'm eyeballing the full-coverage panties with a disturbing amount of excitement. It's come to this—granny panties. Apparently, I'm right on trend. They're all the rage with the hipsters who find them to be panty perfection with those high-waisted pants we once called Mom Jeans. Everything comes back around eventually. Suddenly the thing we all thought of as hideous seems fresh and fashionable again.

Back in my 20s, when I wore leggings as pants without shame, a thong kept the dreaded VPL (visible panty lines) at bay. At the time, the thicker stretch lace back won over the string, and I stuffed my lingerie drawer with an array of alluring thongs with matching push-up bras and camisoles. I modeled underwear and lingerie for a series of print ads for a San Jose lingerie shop. I amassed a collection of vintage cone bras, merry widows, and girdles, which I wore as outerwear to dance clubs, long before Madonna's Blond Ambition Tour. My panty drawer overfloweth(ed).

At 34, I found myself pregnant and suffering from, ahem, hemorrhoids. My posterior expanded along with my midsection. Suddenly the thin strip of fabric that had so easily tucked itself between my cheeks when I was a size 2 was no longer even remotely comfortable. Butt floss, anyone? My compromise was a low-slung, hip-hugging model that fully covered my backside. Still sexy, still flirty, still fun, but this model didn't require careful excavation at the end of a long day. Party in the front, business in the back.

At 40, I continued to embrace the hip-hugger, and after losing enough weight to find myself back in a size 4, thongs returned to the rotation. I stocked up on garter belts, stockings, corsets, and more in celebration of the return of my formerly svelte physique! Hooray for saucy undergarments!

In my late 40s, a potent combination of stress, perimeno-pause, and asthma medications sent me back up the size ladder. Thongs bit the dust as I watched size 6 fade into the rearview mirror. Hipsters returned as I rounded the corner to size 8. Then I hit size 10, then 12, then turned 50 and found myself in new territory without a compass. My hipster panties hit me mid-pooch, creating something less like a muffin top and more like a Bundt cake. This cake was not tasty, not tasty at all. Insert sad face. Pick a pack of panties? Meh.

I found myself wandering through the lingerie department in search of something appealing that bridged the gap between hip hipsters and sad granny panties. On my final visit to a famous purveyor of women's undergarments, a snobby sales-person made it painfully clear that I was no longer the store's target demographic. After so many years of lingerie drawers filled with their lacy bras and undies, the sound of the door hitting me on my size 12, over-50 rear end was deafening. Hey, Victoria. I've got a secret for you. Women want to feel sexy no matter what their size or age.

I'm not suggesting that you can't wear a thong or a hipster or a boy short, or whatever kind of panty you prefer, if you're over 50 and wear a size, 10, 12, or 18. I'm merely stating that I am no longer comfy in a thong or a hipster or a boy short. Until I begin my journey back to a smaller size, I'm weighing my underwear options. I want to put on my big girl panties and get over it, but I wish someone would grasp that a full-coverage panty can still possess stylish details. Where is the saucy granny, the sexy senior, the mischievous matron? Why can't full-coverage panties be sassy, like me? Is that asking too much?

GIRL MEETS SWEATER: A LOVE STORY ... WITH A TWIST!

Once a chill hits the air and my cup magically fills with pumpkin spice coffee, I begin my unrelenting search for the perfect sweater. I have specific needs that I am asking a sweater to meet, a checklist if you will. It looks something like this:

- Comfortable, yet stylish.
- Grazes posterior without accentuating the negative.
- Sneeze-inducing fibers need not apply. That means you mohair, angora, and alpaca. Sorry.
- Fun without being obnoxious, unless it's a Halloween or Christmas sweater, in which case, break out the BeDazzler™!
- Easy to put on and remove as body temperature fluctuates.
- Armholes wide enough to accommodate a human female arm. No straining seams or squished biceps, please.
- Three-quarter-length sleeves preferred, but will entertain wrist length during the coldest months.
- Available in a tasteful array of colors, allowing the wearer to purchase multiples.
- Pill-, fuzz-, and overstretch-resistant.
- Versatile enough to take you from the office to dinner with ease.

Last year, near the end of sweater season, after an exhaustive search, I found the perfect sweater at Goodwill. Imagine my delight as I slipped my arms into the sleeves of a soft, luxurious, mid-calf-length, textured, black, kimono-style cardigan. It had everything and so much more! The only small flaw was a missing belt, but I carefully removed the belt loops with scissors and all was well. I was smitten, so much so that I wore this new-to-me sweater to family gatherings, on shopping excursions, and out to dinner, all the while feeling cozy, chic, and stylish.

Oh sweater, my sweater, how do I love thee? So much!

I decided to search the internet, on the off chance that this sumptuous chenille sweater might be available in other colors. It was then that my unbridled joy came smack up against a most unfortunate truth. This glorious sweater I'd worn hither and yon was a glorious bathrobe.

Wait, what? How could this be? It was clearly placed in the sweater section at the thrift store. I was flimflammed and finagled by the capricious thrift-shop gods. This sweater was not a sweater at all. I was a bathrobe-wearing trashionista.

I dug this bathrobe-posing-as-the-perfect-sweater out of my winter clothes bins this past weekend. The soft, supple, chic simplicity beckoned, dared me to defy convention. Could I? Should I? Would I flout the unspoken laws of fashion and wear a bathrobe as a sweater without shame?

Oh yes, yes I could, should, and will. Now that I've crossed over to the dark side, I'm seriously considering the possibilities of silk pajamas as daywear. Where did I put my turban and marabou slippers?

RANDOM FASHION MUSINGS

Leggings, as pants

What does it matter if women wish to wear leggings as pants? They're freaking comfortable. Don't like it, avert your eyes. On a side note, dear leggings manufacturers, please make leggings a skootch less sheer. In case you have not heard, women are wearing them as pants. Thank you.

High heels

A man invented high heels. This is not shocking. If men had to walk in these torture devices, they'd have gone out of style ages ago. (Actually, heels were invented for men, and, as you can see, they went out of style ages ago—for them.) I'm not sure what this says about women. They do make legs look longer and elevate the saggy parts. I have a love/hate relationship with high heels. I love them, they hate me. We've made a mostly amicable separation, with visitation rights.

Waxing down there

When did women have to add waxing all of the hair from their genitalia to their beauty regimen? Don't we have enough to do already? Is it just me, or does this seem more than a little creepy and also, quite frankly, painful? I've decided to rock a mostly maintained topiary, but I'm seriously considering letting it go and rock a '70s porn bush, because I'm a rebel like that. Bow chicka bow bow.

Lady pants

A few years ago I discovered the holy grail of leggings at Target in the shapewear aisle. I purchased two pairs of these architectural wonders. I dubbed them "lady pants." They lifted, they smoothed, and they were comfortable: the trifecta. When I slid them over my posterior and waistline, a chorus of angels sang *Hosanna in the Highest*. My daughter mocked my lady pants, until she tried them on one day. I now have one pair of lady pants. The other has disappeared. She swears she has no idea what happened to them. I went to replace the missing pair and discovered that they stopped making lady pants. I have not recovered.

Jeans

There is nothing more depressing than shopping for jeans, except shopping for bathing suits. It doesn't matter what size or age you are, because jeans do not discriminate. They're all equally unflattering and ill fitting. The same size jeans at the same store vary wildly from pair to pair. I vote that we categorically reject jeans and replace them with leggings. This is a radical idea and unlikely to gain traction, but a girl can hope, can't she?

Socks

Why can't they make socks without seams or, at the very least, why can't they make the seams face outward? Is there anything quite as irritating as a sock seam rubbing relentlessly across your pinky toe? Even worse, what fool came up with toe socks? Ten seams are ten times as irritating.

Flip-flops

Yes, they're loud, tacky, and designed for shuffling across a boardwalk, but they're so comfortable! This is why they've infiltrated fashion with a relentless, unapologetic assault. I'm convinced that the addition of a judicious smattering of rhinestones, or festive marabou trim, helps elevate them, but I am deluding myself. I like to pair them with leggings as pants for the win. I'm still searching for the winter version of flip-flops. The struggle is real.

Hats

I think we should bring hats back. They are the perfect antidotes for a bad hair day. They instantly elevate even the most mundane outfits. They keep your head warm on a cold day, dry on a wet day, and prevent your hair from flying into your lip gloss on a windy day. While we're extolling the virtues of hats, I'd also like to make a case for wigs.

Wigs

One can be completely transformed in an instant with a wig, avoiding hours at the beauty salon or struggling with hair styling tools. Long hair, short hair, black hair, blue hair, you can have it all and change it on a whim. Be a woman of mystery and intrigue, keep your friends and family guessing. Does she, or doesn't she? Wouldn't they like to know.

Bras

I am not a fan of bras. That's perhaps putting it mildly. I detest bras. What sadist invented the bra? To add insult to injury, recent studies have shown that bras do nothing to keep breasts from sagging. Still, they do lift, separate, and create the illusion of perkiness. If only someone could make the lady pants of bras.

Caftans

I would like to argue that the caftan is the greatest fashion invention of all time. Nothing is more effortlessly chic and deliciously comfortable. A caftan hides a multitude of sins without making you feel like you're wearing a circus tent. Wearing a caftan instantly transports you to an exotic locale, where tasty beverages are delivered in pineapples by scantily clad cabana boys. Who couldn't get behind that initiative?

Pajama pants

I have a dream. It is a simple dream, but a powerful one. In my dream, pajama pants would become a daywear staple. That's crazy!, you say. It would never work!, you say. Pajamas are not pants!, you say. Well, neither are leggings, but who cares? Everyone looks good in pajama pants. Is it a crime to want to be comfortable and stylish? If so, then lock me up in a pair of striped pajama pants and leave me to my foolish dreams.

SLUTTY PILGRIM COSTUMES

I found a dress at Goodwill a while ago. It was one of those super scores that make me super happy. From Anthropologie, with tags, never worn, a $120 dress for a couple of bucks. How this dress made it to our Goodwill, I will never know. It was my intention to sell it, but then I tried it on, it fit, and I liked it. So I kept it. Only later did I realize the zipper was not sewn in properly. It was nothing a few safety pins couldn't fix. I would sew it, but I've got other fish to fry. Or crafts to craft. Or something like that. Insert excuse for not sewing small opening around zipper. . . .

Yesterday, I decided to wear this dress for a TV airing. I realized, rather quickly, that the décolletage was, shall we say, ample. Or, more aptly, this seemingly demure dress was actually seriously saucy. I was running out of time, so I just went with it. I don't feel saucy all that often these days. That afternoon in the car when my daughter saw the dress from behind, she asked me why I was wearing a pilgrim dress.

"Uh, it's fall, and I was on TV."

"Oh, huh."

"Except, the front isn't really very pilgrim."

"It's not?"

"Nope, it's more 'slutty pilgrim.'"

"Is that a thing?"

"I don't know, Google it."

When I got home, I did, in fact, Google it.

I found a dazzling array of slutty pilgrim costumes. Good Lord. Are they serious? Nothing says "I'm gonna sex you up" more than a ruffled bonnet and pantaloons. Am I right?

More disturbingly, these costumes are not intended for Halloween. Oh no! These are for Thanksgiving.

I don't know about you, but I sure love to dress up as a slutty pilgrim for Thanksgiving. Sometimes I dress up as a slutty pilgrim just to clean house or bake cookies or run errands. Why, I've been known to dress up as a slutty pilgrim in the middle of July, just for the heck of it.

There are slutty costumes for everything. Put a word between *slutty* and *costume* and you will probably find a costume for it. What's up with that?

Does it really matter to me?

To be quite honest, it doesn't matter to me in the least. Women should do what makes them happy. What someone else wears or does not wear or chooses to do or does not choose to do really isn't any of my business. I have enough to worry about just wading through my own vast and seemingly endless sea of choices. Live and let live.

If a gal wants to dress like a slutty pilgrim, good for her. Whatever bastes your turkey, sister.

THE TAO OF THE THREE KINDS OF SHOES

There are three kinds of shoes:

Fuck me shoes.

Fuck you shoes.

Don't fuck with me shoes.

Wear the second or third kind to all family functions, except weddings if you're single. In which case, the first kind works best.

There are two distinct contingents—girls who love shoes and girls who just don't get it. Those who just don't get it claim to walk around mostly barefoot or wear sensible, comfortable footwear. Which makes me wonder: If shoes are, in fact, subconsciously tied to our female sexuality, what does that mean to the girl in the comfortable shoes? Is she comfortable with who she is or is she stuck in a rut? Has she ditched her passions for security or has she focused them elsewhere? Is she trying to blend in or is she just tired of having sore feet? Has her libido taken a hike in stilettos, is it hibernating in fuzzy slippers, or is it just fine and not in need of anything thankyouverymuchforasking?

Is the girl who lusts after pricey designer pumps lacking in lust in her bedroom? Is her insatiable desire for fancy footwear a ruse to cover her insatiable longing for love? Are "Fuck me" shoes a way to make us conform to archaic stereotypes of how women should look and walk? Are we desperately seeking saucy or do we bring the saucy to the shoes?

Do we define ourselves by our footwear or does our footwear define us?

Is there a right answer or a wrong answer to these questions?

Why do I feel so Carrie Bradshaw? Is it the shoes? Is it these questions I keep asking and not really answering? Is it my curly mane that I've yet to flat-iron this week?

Even a girl with comfy shoes is still attaching meaning to her footwear on some level. If not, she'd be the girl in the bare feet. My Amish neighbors take off their shoes at the first flush of spring and they don't put them back on until the first frost. They live outside of the shoe continuum; the only meaning their shoes have is to offer protection from the elements. I can't say that's a reflection of their sexual proclivities because they are definitely having sex since they're popping out babies left and right.

A girl who buys Birkenstock, Naot®, Ugg®, and rubber flip-flops is still buying shoes and attaching importance to them—they're just a shoe of a different color. I love comfy shoes, but I also love stylish shoes.

I save saucy shoes for cocktail parties, special events, public appearances, and TV. If I must walk, I shove them in my giant purse and wear comfy shoes until I arrive at my destination.

I am going to go out on a limb here and say that "Don't fuck with me" and "Fuck you" shoes are almost always comfy. They're about saying screw you to convention and stereotypes. My favorite pair of "Don't fuck with me" shoes were my Creepers with the three-inch crepe sole. They made me super tall, super skinny, and super badass. They were also insanely comfy. Conversely, a pair of laced, grommet-, and/or buckle-embellished knee- or thigh-high boots can fall into this category if one wishes to be fucked but not fucked with.

The "Fuck you" shoes I wore until they got a hole in the bottom were a pair of French army boots I purchased at a flea market in Santa Cruz. I laced them with satin ribbons and wore them with frilly dresses. They were ironic in their simultaneous hideousness and slight nod to femininity. I had an entire collection of men's shoes back then, which all had various bows and ribbons placed on them. I liked the androgynous appeal of these shoes immensely.

Back in my day, I could sport my "Fuck me" shoes everywhere, but those days are long, long gone. Traipsing around town in five-inch heels is better left to 20-somethings; now I wear them when I can sit my aging fanny on a stool and cross my legs seductively. The fact is, they make me feel happy, and it has little or nothing to do with anyone else. On one level they are meant to attract, but on another they aren't. Ah, the dichotomy.

Come here, come here, come here . . . go away, go away, go away.

In the Hans Christian Andersen version of "The Red Shoes," a girl wears a pair of red shoes that initially brings her joy and eventually entraps her because she is "vain and self-absorbed." Or is she? She can get the red shoes off her feet only when she repents. She must admit that it was wrong to want to own pretty shoes. She must become plain and dull and stop trying to stick out from the crowd. She's a bad, bad girl and she must see the way.

That is a powerful story, but perhaps not for its intended message. It's powerful because it reinforces the idea that women who try to stand out are bad. Women who want to wear red shoes are bad. Women who wish to pamper themselves are self-ish and vain. The story isn't about the shoes as much as it is about the message that we are not supposed to rock the boat.

I think women should wear shoes that make them feel good. If that's comfy shoes or no shoes or sexy shoes . . . it matters little. As long as we are wearing shoes for us and not for everyone else, our shoes are saying that we are in control and in charge and we don't give a fuck if you don't like them. We can wear whatever shoes please us.

And remember that the slippers Dorothy wore were red . . . and sparkly . . . and magical. They protected her from evil and took her home.

EIGHT *flabby*

D IS FOR DIET

PLUS SIZE

I think our cultural obsession with being skinny (which has morphed into an obsession with muscular arms, ample bosoms, tiny waists, rounded bottoms, waif-thin thighs, and six-pack abs) is making most of us miserable. It isn't doing younger women any favors, either.

What does "plus size" mean anyway? Plus what, puberty?

The average size of a woman in America is 14. Yet, that's where "plus size" begins. If we must quantify sizes, how about we consider "minus size" or "half size" or "curvalicious" or "extra awesome"? Or, better yet, how about we just have a variety of sizes and stop feeling the need to categorize them?

I spent most of my life as a skinny person. I was the kind of person who could eat whatever she liked and never get fat. I shopped in the juniors department because I was too small to fit into women's sizes. I once complained to my local Target that they needed to carry more clothes in size extra-small. Yes, I was that person. My weight fluctuated within a range of 5 pounds or so. After I had my daughter in my mid-30s, I gained 50 pounds. After giving birth, nursing, and a little diet and exercise, I got down to a size 4. Then something shifted around the age of 45. With the combination of stress, less activity, metabolism

shifts, hormones, and medications, I found myself gaining copious amounts of weight. My body has not been cooperating with
my efforts to lose copious amounts of weight. I am learning to
embrace myself at this size and let go of the weird attachment
I had to the smaller, more svelte me. This has not been easy. I've
been conditioned to believe that being thinner makes me prettier. The fashion industry refuses to create clothes that flatter
fuller figures. The media celebrates the slender and denigrates
the curvy. The messaging is loud, clear, and relentless.

Women come in all shapes and sizes and all of them are
beautiful, exactly as they are. There is no "one size fits all" for
beauty and there shouldn't be. Curves are beautiful. All sizes
and shapes are beautiful.

> **WE TELL A** lot of stories in our culture about
> women and their bodies, about what is beautiful,
> what is ugly, what is acceptable, and what is
> not acceptable, and every time we hear one of
> these stories it chips away at our self-worth.
> We need to start telling another story.

Young women face a world that is hyper-obsessed with
appearances at the expense of what is real. It is harder for them
than it was for our generation, because we weren't living on
the internet every minute of the day, posting photos and pray-
ing for likes. We weren't living our lives under an increasingly
cruel and unreasonable microscope. What can all women do
to fight these limiting narratives and shift the dialogue? We
can start by not participating in negative discourse. We can
refrain from making the offhanded, mean-spirited, attention-

seeking comments about celebrities or women we see as we move through the world. We can shut those thoughts down and replace them with positive, uplifting, expansive thoughts instead. If more of us stand up for other women and their right to be exactly who they are, wear what they please, say what they think, and live their lives as they see fit, the story will begin to shift. Let's change the story. We can do that, together.

THE D WORD

Coffee must be steaming black,
Dessert carts will be ushered back.
Chocolate is your enemy,
Stevia your frenemy.
Burgers, fries, and apple pies,
Become a threat to slimming thighs.
Lettuce eat, your rallying cry.
No more candy, said with a sigh.
No wine? You whine,
Have you lost your mind?
Water, water everywhere,
And not a martini to drink!
What fresh hell is this?
Something is amiss.
Who could ever love a diet?
Not I, that's why I'll never try it.

RANDOM THOUGHTS ON FOOD AND DIETING

When I was a teenager, I went on the popcorn diet. No one suggested this diet; I figured it out all by myself.

Step right up and get the revolutionary new Popcorn Diet. It's fairly simple—just replace two meals a day with popcorn. Popcorn has no caloric value. If you use an air popper, it's a net loss. I lost weight, but I spent a lot of time flossing. The downside to this diet is that popcorn popped in an air popper tastes like Styrofoam. As you can imagine, this diet didn't last long. Now I can't eat popcorn without melted butter and shredded extra-sharp cheddar cheese.

I have managed to ruin a lot of good-for-me foods over the years. After all, if it's tasty, wouldn't it be tastier dipped in a flavorful sauce or sprinkled generously with a yummy topping? Why stop at tasty when you can create a mouth explosion?

These are rhetorical questions.

I was much less food adventurous as a child because I have a visceral dislike of mayonnaise. When my mother was pregnant with me, she could not eat mayo. Even in utero I was protesting the ingestion of that vile substance. I won't even spread it on my husband's sandwiches—I hand him the jar with a look of disgust and turn away. Just thinking about mayo makes me gag.

My limited childhood powers of deduction led me to believe that anything that resembled mayo was suspect. This meant I avoided a wide variety of sauces and toppings. It took me years to figure out that sour cream was delicious. Then I discovered the culinary delights of hollandaise and béarnaise sauces. After that I dug into yogurt, ranch and blue cheese dressings, and cottage cheese. There was a world of wonders to explore!

My kryptonite is onion dip. There are two onion dips that I savor, Lipton® Onion Soup Mix mixed with full fat sour cream or Heluva Good!® French Onion Dip. I am particular when it comes to onion dip. Don't try to slip me some no-name generic brand. I don't dip vegetables in my onion dip, even though it might be marginally healthier. Why ruin a perfectly good onion dip with vegetables? I like my onion dip served straight up with a generous helping of Ruffles® potato chips. I like what I like, folks. My relentless specificity is an ongoing struggle that I have passed on to my daughter, along with pale skin, a preternatural distaste for mayonnaise, and a subversive sense of humor. She also hates onions, but she loves onion dip. Go figure.

Though I have developed a hearty love of sauces, you can't fool me with tartar sauce or Thousand Island dressing. Somehow, some fool managed to make mayonnaise even more disgusting. What the hell is wrong with these people? Have they no sense of decency?

I still can't believe how many years I went without knowing the wonders of crème brûlée.

I think everything is better with butter. Therefore, Julia Child is my idol.

On the Atkins diet I could enjoy all of the meats, eggs, sauces, and dips that I wanted, but none of the crunchy delicious carbohydrates. I lost weight, but I cried a lot. I decided my happiness was more important than having a smaller posterior. Butter up that bread, baby!

My favorite food group is orange. Cheez-Its®, Cheez Doodles®, cheese balls, cheese, orange soda, orange juice, so much to love! Orange is such a happy color. Plus, cheese is my favorite.

I have a friend from China. She once told me that the Chinese don't eat cheese because they think it makes you violent. I lobbed a cheese stick at her. That shut her up.

NOBODY LIKES KALE

Nobody likes kale. Sure, they will tell you that they LOVE kale. They will insist that kale is delicious, a perfect food bursting with nutrition, and they love to eat it every day. They will become seriously offended if you suggest that kale is not delicious. "You just don't understand," they'll say. "Kale is the BEST."

Uh-huh.

I say kale is the Emperor's New Clothes of food. People say they love it, but they're lying. If they're not lying, they've been brainwashed. They've lost their ever-loving minds. Their taste buds have gone awry. Nobody likes kale; they love the idea of kale. They love the idea so much that they've convinced themselves that they love kale. What they really love is the feeling of superiority that eating kale gives them. They love the idea of appearing healthier than the other slobs while drinking gloopy, bitter, decidedly untasty green juice, crunching on hideously horrid kale chips, and wearing yoga pants in public.

Kale may be healthy, but it is not tasty. It will never, ever be tasty. It is the crap they put under the orange slice on your plate at Denny's®. It may be filled with minerals, but rocks are also filled with minerals and we don't eat them for dinner. Whoever masterminded the marketing behind kale is a genius. They should be given an award and immediately hired to market other "good for you" but unappealing things like the DMV or colonoscopies.

There are kale shortages right now. People are so bamboozled by the lies perpetuated by the Kale Marketing Association that they've bought up all of the kale. It's insanity!

There are kale chips, kale smoothies, kale candies . . . yes, kale candies—blech. There is even kale ice cream. The horror! Who would do such a thing to delicious ice cream? What is happening in this world?

Someone has to say it and it might as well be me.

Nobody likes kale.

MY CHEEZ-IT PROBLEM

I'm not sure if you should trust a person who doesn't like Cheez-Its.

My daughter came home from school one day to find me sitting in my studio with an empty box beside me, telltale orange crumbs across the front of my white ribbed cotton tank top, a glazed expression on my face. She picked the box up and shook it. She gave me an irritated look.

"WHAT HAPPENED TO THE CHEEZ-ITS?!"

I smiled slyly, holding the box up to cover my shame-filled face and replied in my sweetest of voices . . .

"I have a little problem."

It's true, it's true!

I think they're evil. They may claim it's paprika in them there orange squares, but methinks it's something a bit more powerful. Something so powerful I simply cannot stop popping them into my mouth. Pop, pop, pop. Holy crap! I ate the whole freaking box!

I must ignore the siren call of the orange and red box. I must not think of the crunchy snap between my two front teeth. I must forget the salty goodness on the tip of my tongue and the tang of cheddar as it dances gleefully across my taste buds.

I must remember that a serving is a mere 20 crackers.

I must resist . . .
the siren song
. . . of the Cheez-It.
Do you think they have a 12-step program?

THE FIVE STAGES OF A DIET

Most diets fail for any number of reasons. Nothing about going on a diet says "fun." First of all, there's no cake. To add insult to injury, ice cream is off the table. Literally. As if that wasn't depressing enough, bread and butter, two of life's greatest pleasures, are also off-limits. You can't even wash down your wilted spinach with a nice Pinot Grigio. It's dismal, but the rewards may outweigh the challenges. Diets aren't for wusses; they require immense amounts of intestinal fortitude. It won't be easy, but if you can make it through the five stages of a diet, you can make it through anything.

STAGE ONE: DENIAL

Diets are all about denial—denying yourself things that you enjoy. Denial is the main reason diets fail. As soon as you tell yourself you can't eat a certain food, it will be all that you think about. It will become an obsession. You will start to notice that everyone is eating this food. This food will appear in every TV show, movie, magazine, and commercial. You will then become paranoid. You will wonder if there's a covert plot to derail your diet. There is—it's being financed by the food industry. They're not fucking around, folks. They've spent billions of dollars engineering food to maximize mouth feel and the ratio of salt/sugar/fat that causes our brains to light up like a Christmas tree. It's not you, it's the food. The deck is stacked in the house's favor.

STAGE TWO: **ANGER**

This is what happens when you start to go into withdrawal. It's not pretty.

"Fucking diets are the worst. I hate lettuce. This green juice sucks. I can't believe these people, eating macaroni and cheese right in front of me. Have they no decency? Don't they know that crap is killing them? I'm going to set them straight. Hey! Do you know how many calories are in that macaroni and cheese? How can you do that to your body? Hey, wait, don't leave yet, I'm not finished!"

During the anger phase, you may find yourself spending a lot of time alone. Nobody likes angry dieters. They're worse than reformed smokers. Get a punching bag and some boxing gloves and channel that anger into exercise.

STAGE THREE: **BARGAINING**

This is the part of the diet where you might slip up a little. You've seen some results, and you're feeling cocky. You tell yourself that if you eat a Snickers® bar today you will eat one more salad tomorrow. Don't do it. It starts with a Snickers bar and before you know it, you're waking up from a food coma on the couch surrounded by wrappers, boxes, and cans. Not that I'd know anything about that, mind you. This is the crossroad—a lonely, sad crossroad. There's no sugarcoating this, and there shouldn't be, because sugar is poison. Hello! Step away from that Snickers bar.

STAGE FOUR: **DEPRESSION**

This is the sad part. The diet may be working, but the thought of eating one more piece of celery is taking away your will to live. There will be tears. There will be protestations. There will be weeping, moaning, and gnashing of teeth. You will be sorely tempted to cheer yourself up with a slice of cake. Cheer yourself up with a new smaller pair of lady pants instead. Look at you, losing weight! Play some sad songs, cry some sad tears, watch some sad movies. You've made it this far. Hang in there, sister.

STAGE FIVE: **ACCEPTANCE**

Somewhere along the way, while you were distracted by a whirlwind of emotions, you lost weight. You look better! You feel better! Clothes fit better! YAY, YOU! This gives you a new sense of purpose and conviction. Use this to propel yourself forward, because you're going to go through these five stages multiple times as you make your way to your goal weight. Eventually, you will arrive at your goal weight, feeling fabulous, wondering how you ever got to that number on the scale. There are those last five pounds, which can prove frustrating, but stay the course. The trick is staying at your new weight, which means the diet will have to segue into a lifestyle change.

I've yet to successfully implement this final phase, but I've heard good things about it.

FEARLESS
FRAZZLED
FORLORN
FLEXIBLE
FLUMMOXED
FLAMBOYANT
FASHIONABLE
FLABBY
FEMINIST
FREE

NINE

feminist

JOIN THE LADY
PARTY—WE HAVE
COCKTAILS

WHATEVER HAPPENED TO THE ERA?

Does anyone remember the Equal Rights Amendment? In case you need a refresher, this is the gist of it:

SECTION 1. Equality of rights under the law shall not be denied or abridged by the United States or by any state on account of sex.

SECTION 2. The Congress shall have the power to enforce, by appropriate legislation, the provisions of this article.

SECTION 3. This amendment shall take effect two years after the date of ratification.

What could possibly be the problem with giving women equal rights? What is the objection to ratifying this innocuous amendment? What are they so afraid of? Whatever it is, the ERA has been ratified by only 35 of the necessary 38 state legislatures since it was passed by Congress in 1972. Even with the extension of the deadline to 1982, the ERA has yet to be fully ratified. The ERA has been presented to every Congress since the second deadline passed, but it has not been passed yet. We have been waiting 36 years for this amendment to be ratified. Women got the right to vote in 1920, and we've been waiting for equal rights ever since.

I'm still waiting. My daughter is waiting. Half of the population of the United States is still waiting to be recognized as having equal rights under the law. But the ERA is rarely discussed these days. Setting women against each other is far more entertaining than encouraging us to join forces and demand equality. A few years back I appeared on a "reality" TV competition show. I was disappointed to discover that the narrative for our episode revolved around the two older women clashing. I was shocked at the behavior of my competitor, who hurled insults at me for hours from across the room. I refused to play the game, and therefore I lost. This is par for the course for cable TV. There are entire TV reality franchises built on pitting women against each other. If you look at the narratives of the housewife shows on cable, they're driven by contrived conflict. Reality TV is manipulated and massaged to produce drama. It's presented as truth, but it's a lie. This female versus female narrative filters into our social media and creeps into our day-to-day interactions. The 2016 presidential election and the shit storm of "fake news" online have divided women even further.

And, of course, bra burning (remember that?), raising our voices, speaking our minds, and protesting—it's all so unladylike. Behold, instead, the Stepfordization of the American woman. Smile pretty, ladies! Distracted by our need to wax our nether regions, shrink our waistlines, and increase the puffiness of our lips, we've been sidetracked, and our attention has been deflected from the importance of fighting for equal pay, equal opportunity, affordable and accessible child care, access to affordable reproductive health care, family leave, and the right to work without being sexually harassed or abused. So much of what has been gained is under threat. We can't sit back and let this downslide continue.

I've thought about this often over the years, gotten fired up, and made some noise. I've blogged, ranted on social media, made videos on YouTube. I haven't done much about it beyond that. I have a litany of excuses . . .

Organizing is so much work. Blech.

I have to spackle my face and pluck my chiskers, folks. Be there in a few.

I've got ADHD. I'm easily distracted by shiny things.

My memory is going. What were we discussing, again?

Oh, look, the internet!

Who doesn't like a cute animal video? Amirite?

Do these lady pants make my ass look big? Never mind, I already know the answer to that question.

There is never a shortage of excuses if you're willing to look for them. Taking action requires effort, and it can be downright isolating and even dangerous if folks around you aren't open to your message. Suffragettes were arrested, beaten, and starved for the right to vote. When they went on hunger strikes to protest, they were force-fed through a tube, which resulted in long-term damage to their physical and mental health. If these women could go through all of that to help get us the right to vote, the least we can do is to demand equal rights under the law. We can even go a few steps further to ensure that every woman, regardless of her skin color, sexual orientation, religious beliefs, age, or ethnicity, gets equal rights under the law. That includes transgender women for the win!

I have officially run out of excuses and cute animal videos. I guess it's time for me to get off my sassy ass and do something. What do you say? Are you in? We can do this, women! Let's get the ERA passed. Let's stop buying into the lie that we're competing with each other for success and start helping each other. Together we can become the rising tide that lifts all boats.

We can do it!

F IS FOR FEMINIST

I'm a feminist. Yes, I said it out loud, in public. EGADS!

I've never shied away from that F-word. I have embraced it, owned it, and lived it to the best of my ability. To me it means believing that women should be treated equally under the law, at work, in society, and in relationships. It means that women should have equal access to the fundamental rights of citizenship. It means women should have control over their bodies and their lives. What could possibly be wrong with such a logical idea?

Somewhere along the way, "feminist" became a dirty word. There is a new generation of women who are, in action, thought, and expression, feminists, but who nevertheless refuse to identify themselves as feminists.

I don't like to be labeled or shoved into a box, either. Identifying as a feminist is only part of who I am, not the totality of how I live my life or define myself in the world. For me, it has meant taking an unpopular stance at times, and being the odd girl out. I'm okay with that, because living out loud and living my truth has released me from the expectation—and the burden—of being liked by everyone. On occasion, this has meant losing jobs, losing friends, and even losing heart—sacrifices I've been willing to make, knowing they might help pave the way for other women to fearlessly make similar choices for themselves.

At the same time, there are aspects of me that are not stereotypically feminist. I like makeup and fashion; I have pink hair, I hate bras, but I've never burned one, and I've been known to use glitter rather liberally. A narrow definition of the word *feminist* limits women. We should be free to be, do, say, wear, think, and believe what we choose and allow other women to do the same. That's the true spirit of feminism.

OLDER WOMAN ALMOST BREAKS GLASS CEILING... AND THEN SHE DOESN'T

My country voted for a man who bragged about sexual assault, made highly sexualized comments about his daughter, mocked the handicapped, ridiculed women for being overweight and unattractive, called Mexicans rapists and drug dealers, threatened Muslims with deportation and targeted surveillance, suggested reinstating Stop and Frisk for people of color, called for his opponent to be locked up, and, worse, encouraged his followers to attack protestors, shared fake news stories from white supremacist sources, and lowered the bar of basic civility and common courtesy through a barrage of insults and late-night Twitter rants. This man won the presidency over a woman with 30 years of experience, a woman who has dedicated her life to public service and improving the lives of women and children. This woman has been at the center of a 30-year smear campaign and multiple multimillion-dollar investigations that have yielded not even a single conviction. She has risen to the occasion after being knocked down again and again. It is obvious who is better qualified for the job.

One day we'll look back and wonder how this happened. Articles and books will be written, and college courses will dissect every aspect of the campaign, and its aftermath, in painstaking detail. What did she do wrong? How could she lose? How could this happen?

I know how this happened. I'm a woman over 50 in a world that wants me to disappear. How can any woman hope to shatter the glass ceiling when women are still not equal under the law? How can a 71-year-old woman be elected to the most important job in the nation when most women over 50 can't even get a job? How dare she!

No one wants to see or listen to an older woman. How many of them do you see on TV, in magazines, or in advertisements for anything other than adult diapers, bone density medications, or vaginal mesh lawsuits? During the presidential campaign, I heard things like "She doesn't smile enough. She smiles too much. She laughs at the wrong things. She's shrill. She's got too many wrinkles. She looks fragile. She lacks stamina." Despite her being the most truthful candidate by far, people found her untrustworthy. Worst of all, she was smarter and more informed on virtually every issue than any other person in the race. Nobody likes a know-it-all, especially if it's a woman.

Sexism and ageism are deeply embedded in our cultural

narrative. One must be over 35 to run for the office of president, but you need a level of experience few people possess at that age. The youngest president was Teddy Roosevelt, who was 42 when he succeeded William McKinley. Most of our presidents have been older than 50 when they were elected. This presents some challenges for female candidates. As we know, men become distinguished as they age, and women just get older.

Do I think that gender and age were the only factors in Hillary Clinton's defeat? Absolutely not. But I do think they played a substantial role. There was obviously a lot more at play. While 94 percent of African-American women voted for Hillary, I was seriously disturbed to discover that 53 percent of white women voted for Donald Trump. Breaking that down further, 51 percent of college-educated women voted for Clinton, while 62 percent of women without a college degree voted for Trump. Damn it, white women, get your shit together. White men overwhelmingly voted for Trump across demographics, which is also disturbing, though not shocking.

Hillary Clinton's age, sex, intellect, and income bracket, combined with the media-manipulated (and Russian influenced) narrative about her "trust factor," conspired to defeat her. Regardless of how you feel about Hillary, it's hard to deny that she was held to a completely different standard as a candidate. Trump just had to show up and speak in partial sentences. Hillary, on the other hand, had to show up, smile just the right amount, ignore Trump's barrage of insults and abuses without responding in anger, and articulate her thoughts and positions with authority and detail. Then there were the endless questions about Hillary's emails, while Trump's ties to Russia, lawsuits against him and his company, and sexual assault accusations elicited little of the media scrutiny and moral outrage that dogged Hillary's campaign, and which defeated her in the end.

Will a woman ever be president? I think so. I hope it happens in my lifetime. I cried when I voted, knowing what it took for women to get there. That the glass ceiling is cracking sends a powerful message. Someday soon, I hope, a brilliant, capable, kick-ass woman will take a sledgehammer to that ceiling and shatter it once and for all. When that day comes, it will be a victory for everyone.

GLASS CEILING

We came close, 18 million cracks,
And then they rolled our progress back.
They crowned a predator-in-chief,
We suffered from collective grief.

Calm down, get back, shut up, they cried,
No birth control, no equal rights!
Education? Not for the masses,
That's reserved for the upper classes.

The alt-right's misogynistic bent,
Fueled our Twitter happy president.
Grab 'em by the pussy, smack 'em in the face!
Teach 'em to be quiet, make 'em learn their place.

Women should be seen, not heard,
Girls in STEM? Well, that's absurd.
Let them focus on giving birth,
We'll be the judge of their self-worth.

African Americans, progressives, Mexicans,
LGBTQ, women, and Muslims,
The poor, the handicapped, the tempest-tossed,
Dismissed, demeaned, rejected, mocked.

Immigrants and refugees
Were banished with impunity,
Earmarked as enemies of state,
The focus of misdirected hate.

Every freedom, right, and liberty,
The thin veneer of civility,
Truths held to be self-evident,
Under siege by our new president.

We knitted hats, we painted signs,
Laced up our boots and spoke our minds.
We will not break, we will not bend,
You will not silence us again.

We marched for freedom and equal rights,
We joined hands to stand and fight.
"Hear our voice!" our rallying cry,
Stronger together, watch us rise.

PANDORA'S HOPE: RECLAIMING
THE DIVINE FEMININE

I think we, the collective we, the religious we, the secular we, the political we, the social we, do an endless amount of bending, twisting, and lying to accommodate the male sexual and aggressive impulse. Let's start with Genesis, the first book of the Old Testament, which, among other stories, tells the tale of a man who was so weak and incapable of making his own decisions that a serpent and a woman tricked him. The original sin was not that man chose to eat from the tree of the knowledge of good and evil, it was that woman "forced him" to eat that fruit by merely suggesting he give it a try. That fruit was a metaphor. Eve was the first temptress.

It wasn't his fault.

Eve introduced sin into the world. Adam just went along for the ride. In actuality, the serpent convinced her to eat it. Note that the Genesis mythology was a restructuring of more ancient religious stories where the female was the deity and the serpent her consort. Note that to know the goddess intimately, personally, intrinsically meant eating from her tree of knowledge, knowing her in the carnal, magical, deepest sense. The mysteries of the universe and the divine were discovered through sexual contact. So, even the metaphor of the tree of the knowledge of good and evil was recast in Genesis. In earlier texts, from which the Old Testament was formed, Jahweh had a wife, Asherah, which means "sacred tree." Asherah represented the female experience of the divine. Her name also means "womb." She was often depicted with serpents. These stories, in the Judeo-Christian Bible and in all of the religious texts of the world's major religions, evolved over time and were edited to shape a new mythology.

I've often pondered why Jahweh put that tree in the garden and then made such a big deal about warning Adam and Eve not to eat it. It seems like a setup to me. Also, what's up with the serpent? How did he get in there? What was the point of giving them paradise and then stacking the deck so heavily against them? Also, what's so bad about wisdom, exactly? Is blissful ignorance really paradise? If it is, I'll take a pass.

The message relayed from this story, even if it wasn't fully supported by the text, was that woman was inferior. Therefore, she needed to be forced into subjugation. How better to subjugate woman than to recast her as the enemy? How better to recast the once-powerful goddess than to make her a vessel for male release? Then every woman became, by proxy, a vessel for male release. How better to exert male superiority than to create a new mythology that absolved men from responsibility for their sexual urges and their aggressive impulses?

Woman was weak because she chose to eat the fruit and evil because she convinced man to make the same choice. Man was the hapless victim. By casting women as the agents of the downfall of humanity, we have created a world in which women will always be perceived as duplicitous, dangerous, and inferior. Our current geopolitical reality is the endgame of this mythology.

LGBTQ people are also considered threatening, because they defy the male/female duality. The myth of the male as superior and woman as his servant, vessel, and property is shattered by people who exist outside of this mythology. Marriage began and still exists in many cultures, as a transaction, a way of treating women as property to be handed from one male figure to another. In that sense, marriage as a contract between two equal adults who are not tethered by the patriarchal construct is a threat to the continuation of that mythology. The frantic efforts in this country to enforce religious mythology as law are a direct response to the tide of LGBTQ people who have risen from the shadows and demanded to be treated as equals. By pushing them back down through laws or force, the patriarchal male/female superior/inferior good/evil duality remains unchallenged and unchanged.

It's not just the Judeo-Christian mythology. These underlying male/female themes are present in every major religion. This mythology that men are not responsible, are victims of female temptation, has influenced cultures that regularly subjugate women while blaming them for the male sexual impulse for centuries. This includes Islam, Hinduism, Buddhism, and all of the world's major religions.

The fascinating thing is that so many women have bought into these limiting constructs and accepted a position of inferiority. We have turned myth into reality. We have co-created a world where male sexual and aggressive impulses reign supreme. Whether it means hiding ourselves under layers of fabric, remaining pressed against the glass ceiling, forcing other women to accept the patriarchal code, making ourselves smaller and more docile, allowing physical or sexual abuse, or telling ourselves the story that women are less than, it all contributes to the continuation and proliferation of the mythology.

I believe that we will not find balance between male and female energy until we shift our mythology. We will not find this balance until we stop creating and accepting a reality that tells the story that men cannot control themselves and women are to blame. We will not find balance until we stop telling women how to dress, how to act, what to say, what they can and cannot do with their bodies, how to move through the world as if they are constantly forcing men to think bad thoughts and do bad things. We will not find balance until we create true equality for the sexes. We will also not progress until women stop tearing each other apart and start lifting each other up instead. That's important, because it's a huge hurdle that needs addressing and eliminating. Women cannot rise until they do it collectively.

Each year 20.9 million adults and children are sold into sexual slavery. About 98% of them are female. This is all because we have accepted the myth that men are entitled to sex and women are obligated to provide it regardless of their willingness to comply. This is our great, mostly unspoken, collective shame. These women and children often come from extreme poverty; children are sold out of desperation or tricked into slavery through false promises. In this twisted reality, a virgin is a trophy, not a living, breathing, human being, not a child in need of protecting. This industry exists solely to serve male sexual desire. Despite our cultural taboos regarding the sexual abuse of children, millions of them are sexually abused every single day.

Interestingly, in the Old Testament of the Judeo-Christian Bible, there are multiple passages where Jahweh instructs men to rape, murder, and even tear pregnant women and their unborn fetuses apart if they are women who belong to their enemies. The Bible offers advice on how to force female children into sexual slavery. When so many treat this ancient text as the word of God, it becomes easy to see how what should be unconscionable becomes quietly acceptable.

It isn't just biblical or religious mythology that formed this archetype of woman as evil. The Greek myth of Pandora, the first human woman, also contributes to this idea. Men were immortal, living in a world without women, until Prometheus stole fire from the gods. Pandora was created as a punishment for this act, designed as a "beautiful evil." She was fashioned to lure mankind into sexual congress to create the offspring that would torment the human race. Woman was designed specifically and carefully to bring the downfall of mankind. Her box or jar, like the grail, was opened unleashing evil into the world. Again, woman is to blame. Sure, Prometheus stole fire, but Pandora opened the jar. Yet, interestingly, the only thing remaining inside the jar is hope.

Progress for women's rights has been made, but it is rapidly being lost. Increasing assaults by governments around the world on women's reproductive control all stems from the idea that women are inferior. Controlling women's reproduction allows for the continuation of cycles of poverty and hopelessness. When women are forced to provide sex to men even under force, prevented from using birth control to prevent unwanted pregnancies, and denied access to abortions, women do not have any control over their destiny or even their day-to-day reality.

Shifting this mythology doesn't mean emasculating men, it means asking them to take responsibility for their thoughts, impulses, and actions. It means no longer placing the burden and the blame for male lack of physical control on women. It also means women will have to cease seeing each other as enemies competing for the male gaze or male-dominated cultural approval. When your value stems from your physical attractiveness, you are objectified and lessened. Shifting this mythology also means accepting and embracing the complex spectrum of sexuality as a part of our natural biology and embracing all of the endless variations of being in the world.

I used to think that if women had an equal share in ruling the world, it would be a better world. I still think this, but many of the women who rise to power within the limitations of the patriarchal construct are most often still acting under those rules and limitations. They are still promoting the agenda of the oppressor. I often hear women suggest that if we passed the ERA, women should be forced to sign up for the draft. I find this unacceptable. Equality does not mean indistinguishable or interchangeable. War is unacceptable to me, it is a male construct. I don't think anyone should be forced to sign up for the draft or to fight for the financial gains of the profiteers behind the military-industrial complex. If we pass the ERA, perhaps we should work to end the construct of war. Perhaps then we would work toward a society in the United States and even more importantly, globally, where women's rights are considered human rights and war, rape, violence, aggression, discrimination, sexism, ageism, racism all become abominations and impossibilities.

If women were free to move from a place of unrestricted power and equality, then I do think we could change the world. I think we'd see less violence, aggression, war, fear, greed, poverty, ignorance, and hoarding of resources. I think we'd see more cooperation, kindness, love, abundance, understanding, and sharing of resources. Perhaps I'm wrong, because the programming of division and competition between women may be too strong to override.

Is it possible that there are enough women who reject the prevailing mythology and messaging? Are there enough of us who are willing to join forces to say no to war, greed, corruption, poverty, discrimination, destruction, and control of women's bodies and choices? Can we, as women, reject the patriarchal construct and spur an evolution of consciousness together? Can we reclaim the divine feminine?

Can we open Pandora's jar again to unleash hope upon the world?

HOW TO DRESS FOR THE RESISTANCE

Being a fashionista and a nasty woman presents a few style challenges. I may be a fierce feminist over 50, but I'm not giving up on my pink hair or my love of lip gloss. If you, too, wish to look fabulous while saving the world from ruin, I've got you covered.

Marching in the wind, rain, fog, and snow means your hairdo can become a hair don't in an instant. Forget the pussyhat, might I suggest a jaunty beret instead? They come in so many colors and they give the rebel a touch of that je ne sais quoi.

Hours of marching take a terrible toll on the tootsies. Take a cue from the military and try a stylish combat boot. We liberal ladies have the right to the trifecta of footwear: style, comfort, and functionality. Don't forget steel toes for extra ass-kicking potential.

Skirts or pants? An age-old question, and one every rebel will have to decide for herself. I'm of the mind that a great pair of jeans is a girl's best friend, but perhaps black tights and an A-line mini are more your cuppa java. You do you, sister.

Pepper spray? Never fear! Toss a water bottle in your clear backpack and a patterned bandanna around your neck. Remove, moisten, and feel that sweet relief.

Don't dismiss the power of a statement T-shirt, especially when tucked under a cozy knit cardigan. What message do you wish to impart without saying a word: #uppity? #nasty? #arewestillprotestingthisshit? Sadly, yes.

Et voilà, Nasty Woman, welcome to the Lady Party!

THE B-WORD

Ah, the B-word.

Every strong, confident, successful woman has felt the sting. Perhaps whispered sharply under someone's breath or shouted out in a fit of rage. This word has power, but the focus of that power is entirely up to you.

I've surely been called that word plenty of times over the years by people who were threatened by my self-confidence and willingness to point out that the emperor has no clothes. Or, more aptly, I have been called that due to my observation that most of the people in charge of making the important decisions lack even the slightest whiff of a clue.

Because, let's face it, they mostly don't. It takes a whole lot of ass kissing and compromise to make it to the top of someone else's ladder. I've never been any good at kissing ass, alas. Would that I could pucker up when the need arises or the ass is presented. I can't help myself—it's impossible for me to stay silent when stupidity is running roughshod over common sense. I can't sit back and watch people abuse their power. I am what one might call an insufferable smarty panties, or a bitch.

Six of one, half a dozen of another . . .

We live in interesting times. In some parts of the world, a woman can be stoned to death for being raped. In this part of the world, she can be shamed into silence or humiliated in public. She can also be told, by an elected official, that her body has a way of shutting "that whole thing" down to prevent her from becoming pregnant. Therefore, if she didn't put up the shutters on her uterus, she must not have been raped. Obviously. We're still not paid the same as a man for doing the same job, one at which we quite likely excel. Many of us balance full-time work with full-time parenting. We won't risk death, but if we speak up or speak out or dare to stand out in any significant way, someone is more than likely going to think or call us the B-word.

I think we have to own it. Being a strong, confident, smart, successful, compassionate, kick-ass, warrior woman isn't something to be feared; it's something to be celebrated. It's up to us to throw the party. We have to be mindful of not getting caught up in the mythology of the strong woman as a negative archetype. That's important for ourselves and also for how we treat other women. Women need to lift each other up, not tear each other down.

And, for the record, just because we're strong doesn't mean we don't like lip gloss or a new pair of shoes. Whether we do or don't is entirely our own business.

The willingness to own your power and to speak and live freely, even if it means risking not being liked, is the key to true happiness. Standing up for yourself and for others, taking the unpopular stand when it's the right thing to do. Fighting the good fight, despite the opposition. Showing the seams, owning the missteps, being transparent and real. You may not win Miss

Congeniality, but really, isn't that just a fancy way of saying best ass kisser? Besides, wouldn't you rather bedazzle your own sash and crown?

Bitch?

That's Ms. Bitch to you.

DEAR GEORGE

This is an imaginary email chain to George Soros. I wrote it after the 2016 Women's March when the buzz on social media suggested the marchers were being paid by Mr. Soros. Obviously, that was fake news.

Dear Mr. Soros,

It's Madge, Margot Potter! May I call you George? I figured it was okay since I just found out that I'm on your payroll. Please make my checks out to Margot Potter. Madge is my nickname. Thank you so much for the job!

Cheers,
Margot

Dear George,

I wanted to keep you updated on my activities. I've been so busy protesting that I've developed a nasty case of shingles.

Speaking of shingles: Do you include health insurance coverage in your paid protestor employment plan? How about workers' compensation? Where do I sign up for those?

If you could send that first check soon, I'd really appreciate it. These antiviral medications aren't cheap.

Cheers,
Margot

Dear George,

How are you? I attached some pics from the March on Washington, for proof of attendance. Thanks so much for the hats. Those "knitters" sure had everyone fooled, eh?

I also attached my travel receipts. I have it billed two ways, since I took a bus. Is it 53.5 cents a mile or the cost of the bus ticket? Please advise.

I'm really looking forward to working together!

Cheers,
Margot

Dear George,

About that check, I wasn't sure if you had the correct address. Should I call your office?

I'm starting to worry that it got lost in the mail.

Cheers,
Margot

Dear George,

I feel as if we're developing a real kinship here. You're such a good listener!

I'm gearing up for the March for Science in April and I was wondering if you had a time line on the brain hats. Can I request a specific color? Are there any messages you feel best represent the spirit of the march? Since global warming is just a scam you created with Al Gore, I figured you might have some great protest sign ideas.

Talk soon,
Margot

Dear George,

I'm not sure my emails are reaching you. Please check your spam folder.

Cheers,
Margot

Dear George,

I realize that you are a busy man. However, participating in the Resistance takes a lot of effort. A little acknowledgment of my contributions would be appreciated.

Impatiently,
Margot

Dear George,

So this is how it is, huh? No checks, no emails, no phone calls . . .
Is this how you treat your paid protestors?

I guess you really do have an exaggerated view of your own self-importance. For the record, I've met the Messiah, and you, sir, are no Messiah.

Well, I haven't met the Messiah, but I do follow him on Twitter.
I have half a mind to stop protesting if this continues.

> Whatever,
> Margot

Dear George,

Please forgive me for my last email; shingles are a bitch. I'm half out of my mind, and yet I'm still conscious enough to be outraged. Maybe outraged isn't the right word. Disgruntled? Yes, that's better.

Anywho, I'm going to have to file for unemployment since it's obvious you're not going to pay me. Thanks for nothing.

> Cheers,
> Margot

JOIN THE LADY PARTY

Ain't no party like a lady party
Can't we all just tie one on?
Sit back and let the ladies handle this
We've got cocktails . . . and opinions
Life, Liberty, and the Pursuit of a Great Pair of Jeans
Because we said so
We're always right, unless we're wrong . . . which is never
Momma knows best
Giving birth is hard, running a country is easy
Ladies first
Yes, she can
Dancing backwards and in high heels since 1933
Step off our skirts
Ladies of Liberty
A woman's place is in the White House
Because bitches get shit done

TEN

free

RELEASING THE WILD WOMAN

WILD WOMAN MANIFESTO

From the moment we become aware, women are taught how to be. We are limited by the world around us, a world that is hostile to the wild woman who lives inside of us. We are told to smooth the edges, hide the seams, follow the rules, act like a lady, and do what we're told. This helps to dissipate the threat from the wild woman. She's dangerous, because she defies the social norms.

Even the "rule breakers" police us from their own limited constructs. "Conform to our version of nonconformity! You're not nonconforming properly!"

We are sent an endless stream of contradictory messages that reinforce the lie that we are not good enough no matter what we choose. The drip, drip, drip wears away at that wild woman, taming her into submission.

Here's a secret: The world may construct the cage, but we lock ourselves inside and hide the key.

This wild woman has had enough. She's setting herself free.

Every aspect of how I live my life and move through the world belongs to me. I don't owe anyone an excuse or an explanation. I don't owe anyone anything at all. I am tired of being policed. In fact, I soundly reject it. I am also tired of policing.

It's not my place to tell other people what to think, do, say, wear, feel, believe. It's not my place to tell other people what to think about me. If the world finds me three notches too loud and five notches too sparkly, that's a judgment. It is only truth if I accept it.

My wild woman is fully unfettered. She will do as she pleases and she does not care if it pleases you. She will wear what she pleases, think what she pleases, and say what she pleases. She will vote as she pleases, love whom she pleases, and live as she pleases. She will age as she pleases. She does not require your approval.

MRS. POTTER REGRETS

I posed a question on Facebook today: "Is there anything in your past you'd like to do over if it were possible to go back and make a different choice?" I asked because there is something I would most definitely like to do over, but since this is not a possibility, I'm working extra hard every day to keep marching forward. Some days are easier than others. Some days I feel as if I'm swimming in concrete.

It is my belief that a life lived fully is bound to contain at least a few regrets. Life is, after all, a series of choices, consequences, and reactions to the consequences of our choices.

Some folks in my thread handed the power over to the Divine, claiming that everything that has happened in their lives was "God's plan." My sincere apologies if this offends, but I don't believe that's true. If it were all destiny, I'd feel like tossing the towel in today. If there is no free will, we would never need to make any choices at all. If it's all part of someone else's plan, we are no longer responsible for any of our choices. In fact, that pesky thing called free will was the problem from the start, wasn't it? We must choose—that's part of the deal.

"Well, officer, I do realize that the car was speeding. Yes, I also know that it ran over several pedestrians, but, you see, I handed the wheel to Jesus. He's a terrible driver, but a top-notch Messiah. So, if you don't mind, you can make that ticket out to Jesus Christ and I'll be on my way."

We can't live our lives playing the "would have, could have, should have" game. We can, however, learn and grow from the consequences of our choices. Life offers us lessons and opportunities for growth, grace, and forgiveness. We can feel remorse and take ownership of the choices that may have led to pain for others. We can learn to trust that still, quiet voice inside that is almost always pointing true north. To take responsibility for the consequences of your choices is a powerful thing and a sobering thing. We can, if we CHOOSE, make different choices with richer and more rewarding consequences. In that sense, what we choose, no matter what the consequences, offers us the same lesson—the opportunity to practice unconditional love.

Is it so wrong to want to learn that lesson with a little less collateral damage?

Does Mrs. Potter regret? Yes, she does regret a few things. She regrets the things left unspoken, and the things spoken in anger or sadness. She regrets a handful of questionable choices and the manner in which they negatively affected people she loves. She regrets the moments she was not present enough, compassionate enough, or thoughtful enough. It's likely that when it's all said and done, there will be a few more.

TOP TEN THINGS
ABOUT WHICH I NO LONGER CARE

1. The Kardashians.

2. Tampons.

3. What other people think about me.

4. Being pretty.

5. Arguing with people on social media.

6. Making the grade.

7. Making myself smaller to make other people happy.

8. Aging gracefully.

9. What's in and what's out.

10. People telling me to smile.

TEN THINGS
ABOUT WHICH I CURRENTLY CARE

1. The future of the world.

2. Comfortable shoes.

3. What I think about myself.

4. Being interested and engaged.

5. Making meaningful connections with nice people.

6. Breaking the rules.

7. Making myself happy.

8. Aging disgracefully.

9. What's real.

10. Surrounding myself with people who inspire me to smile.

BECAUSE YOU'RE WORTH IT

I was at QVC a few years back, being fitted for my microphone before going on air. A man stopped to compliment me on my dress. I started the "Oh this old thing? It's godawful, blah, blah, blah" thing that women do. He smiled and laughed. Then he asked me why it was that women simply cannot accept a compliment without a long-winded list of reasons they don't deserve one?

I have pondered this ever since. It's a very good question. People give us compliments because they genuinely mean them and they want to make us feel good. If we can't graciously accept them, we deprive them of that opportunity. Is it really that tough to wrap our minds around the simple fact that someone finds us attractive, smart, funny, interesting, or worthy of praise?

After that illuminating moment, I broke out of my habit of immediately responding to a compliment with a self-effacing witticism. I shut off the voice inside of me that told me I was unworthy of compliments. Now I breathe them in and feel worthy. Because I am. Worthy. You are worthy. We all are. I love me! What was I thinking?! Whenever I instinctively blurt out something along the lines of "I'm so imperfect they need to invent a new word for it" or "I got this dress on the sale rack. It has a stain on it," I try to regroup and follow that with a simple "Thank you for the lovely compliment."

Sometimes the hardest thing we do in life is to accept that we deserve happiness. We're our own worst enemies. You like me? Me?! Are you freaking kidding? I'm such a dork. You must be a real asshole for liking me. What the hell is wrong with you?! Why don't you go and like someone else?

Until we open our hearts to love, we will never really be able to receive it. If we are unable to receive it, we will be unable to fully love anyone else. Yes, you deserve to be loved. So, start acting like you deserve it, Sweet Cheeks, or soon the compliments are going to dry up like your post-menopausal vagina.

Here's a little dime-store guru advice, for what it's worth. Stand in front of your mirror every morning and pay yourself a sincere compliment. Like "Shazam! You are one hot tamale!" or "Hubba, hubba that's a seriously sassy caboose you've got there" or "Hey, nice blouse. That's a good color for you."

You get the picture.

I am sending all of you a compliment today. I think you're the bee's knees.

Now please don't tell me about your knee surgery.

WRITE A NEW STORY

There was a commercial for an antidepressant medication a while back that featured a black cloud on a string that followed a sad person around. My daughter dubbed it "the depression turd." I loved that! Depression is less of a cloud, and more of an incredibly stinky turd that leaves its stench on everyone and everything, and follows us wherever we go. The more we drag it around, the bigger and smellier it becomes.

You don't have to define yourself by your old stories. You can choose to write a different one: This happened to me then, but this is what I am choosing *now*. Why keep dragging a turd around? You can flush that crap any time you like.

The world is filled with horror. People survive and endure things most of us cannot imagine surviving. We can't ignore these things, but we don't have to focus on them. They can remain in the past, or we can drag them into our present. Every day we make that choice. No matter what we've endured, we can rise above it. We have choices! Happy people aren't in denial of sorrow; they've just opted not to get stuck in it. The truth is, we define our experience of life. Our reality is shaped by our perception and the choices we make.

When you start to feel yourself getting dragged into negativity, breathe deeply, take a moment, and ask yourself, "How is this serving me—or anyone else? Is what I am about to do or say contributing to the greater good?" You are allowed to walk away from negativity. You can remove yourself from people who continuously seek to dull your sparkle. You don't owe them anything at all. You can walk off their set. You don't have to be in their movie. You have the power to write your own story: You can choose an adventure or a mystery, a romance or a thriller, a comedy or a tragedy. And you can, if you so choose, write your own happy ending.

CARPE GAUDIUM

This New Year we rented a little apartment on the River Liffey in the Temple Bar District in Dublin, Ireland. My husband, my daughter, and I spent a week exploring the city together. Now that our daughter is away at college, our trio has become a duet. With the amount of travel my husband does for work, the duet is often a solo act. It was nice to get the old band together again and take the show on the road.

A place called Ink Factory was right next to the entrance to our apartment. It's a tattoo and piercing parlor, barber shop, and coffee purveyor. I'm not even remotely cool enough to hang out there, but they were very welcoming and kind enough to pretend they didn't notice. I've toyed with the idea of getting a tattoo for years. My husband has several. Many of my friends have wildly colorful tattoos running up both arms. Way back in my wayward youth, most of my friends had tattoos. I was never able to decide on anything that I wanted emblazoned on my body forever. I decided to wait until I felt moved enough to do it.

Before we left for Dublin, I decided to go into the New Year actively embracing exciting new experiences. As I'm a writer, and I love words, I decided to get a favorite phrase tattooed on the inside of my left wrist in a vintage-style typewriter font. At the age of 55 my skin is not perfectly smooth; therefore, neither is my tattoo. I'm okay with a little wabi-sabi. My new tattoo says *Carpe Gaudium*. The Latin word *carpe* literally means "pick, pluck, pluck off, cull, crop, gather, serve." The word *gaudium* means "joy." Okay, so work with me here, people. *Carpe* means "seize and serve" and *gaudium* means "joy." When we "seize joy" we can also "serve joy," meaning the act of embracing it for ourselves offers us the opportunity to serve it to others.

What if we seized as much joy as we could carry, as often as possible, and then let it spill out and over and around us to others? How would that inform our experience? How would that shift our perspective?

Seize joy. Share joy. Become happy.

Watch the world shift.

My new tattoo is a reminder, especially at those moments when I lose perspective, that I'm in charge of the journey, the destination, the perspective, and the message I share with others. I choose.

I can, if I so choose, seize joy as often as possible and share that with those I meet along the way.

Carpe gaudium.

BITTERSWEET

Bittersweet is one of my favorite words.

It's encapsulates the complexities of being so succinctly.

Most joy has some element of sorrow. It could be the sorrow of what is missing, or the sorrow of what is yet to be, or the sorrow of wanting to share the experience with someone who is not present, or the sorrow of knowing that joy cannot be sustained.

Being in the moment is so difficult because we carry so much into each moment. We carry the burden of what has passed, and we carry the anticipation of what's to come. This makes being fully engaged and invested in what is happening right now challenging. The moment is all that is real, but moments pass before we can evaluate them. We assign meaning to them in retrospect. We alter them by examining them. Moments are not good or bad, they just are. We view moments through clouded lenses.

As I get older, I find myself reflecting on time: I see the seconds, minutes, hours, days, weeks, months, and years of moments past. I know that what lies behind me is greater than what lies ahead of me. My time is decreasing. This gives new moments a deeper resonance, but that's perspective. The moments to come are no more or less important than the moments that have passed.

I think more often these days about the importance of not wasting moments, yet I waste them anyway. I waste them when I focus on what I don't have, what I have lost, and what I didn't say or do. I waste them waiting for invitation, illumination, affirmation. This is frivolous. My life is a nanosecond in eternity. Most of what I find happy or sad or meaningful is meaningless in the face of infinity.

I know this. Yet, here I am, breathing in, breathing out. Feeling all the feelings. Stretching toward infinity. Aching for meaning. Seeking the purity of the unfettered moment. Feeling the complexity of being alive.

Bittersweet—both pleasant and painful.

Yes, this.

"AGE IS JUST A NUMBER" AND OTHER STUPID THINGS PEOPLE SAY ABOUT GETTING OLD

- **AGE IS JUST A NUMBER.** Sometimes it's a really big number. When the number gets too big, you can't fit all the candles on your birthday cake without having a fire safety professional on call. This adds the perfect touch of danger to the occasion.

- **I'M OLDER AND I KNOW BETTER.** Do you, though? I know a lot of older people. I can attest to the fact that many of them don't know better, as evidenced by how many of them voted for Donald Trump.

- **SHE'S NO SPRING CHICKEN.** I live on a farm. Spring chickens are overrated. Many of them don't make it to summer. Winter chickens are survivors. I propose we create a new saying, "She's a winter chicken—what a plucky broad!"

- **FIFTY IS THE NEW 30.** No, it's not. It's 50. Brown is also not the new black. It's brown.

- **YOUTH IS WASTED ON THE YOUNG.** See "Fifty is the new 30."

- **YOU'RE TOO OLD TO WEAR THAT.** I will wear what pleases me and you can mind your own damn business.

- **SEX, AT YOUR AGE?** Is that an offer or an inquiry? Yes, to both. Thanks!

- **OLD PEOPLE AND TECHNOLOGY, RIGHT?** Would you like my reply via tweet, text, snap, FB post, GIF, meme, email, instant message, or the classic no-tech middle finger?

- **ACT YOUR AGE.** I never have before, why would I start now?

- **IT'S NEVER TOO LATE TO LIVE YOUR DREAMS.** Unless your dream is to be 15, in which case once you turn 16, you're screwed.

EVERYDAY MAGIC

This morning something magical happened. You may not think it was magical. On the surface, it's perhaps even prosaic. Still, I'm a believer in everyday magic.

When we moved this past summer, I misplaced my favorite necklace. After months of searching, I thought for sure it was gone for good. Then this morning, I opened the cabinet that I open about a hundred times a day and saw a red organza bag. I felt compelled to reach in, pick up the bag, and open it. Inside of the bag was a carved quartz cabochon we've had for many years, two big-faceted Swarovski sew-on stones, one tiny blue ceramic tile, a few unused metal stamping blanks . . . and my missing necklace.

Why today? Why after months and months of digging through boxes, bags, bins, and drawers would this necklace finally show up? Was it always there? How did I miss it?

Just a few days ago, I stood in the same room and said to my husband, "Why is it the things we don't care about never seem to get lost? We stumble upon them over and over again in drawers and boxes and wonder why we still have them. Yet, the things that do matter disappear?"

I used to joke that when you die, you get a box. Inside of the box are all the things you lost while you were alive. The box would be filled with keys, jewelry, single socks, tickets, and papers that seemed to have so much resonance when you were frantically looking for them . . . random things that would have no resonance at all once you were dead. This box would show you how absurd and pointless it was to have been so concerned about those things.

As I let go of things that are weighing me down and holding me back, I make room for experiences that will lift me up and propel me forward. I feel lighter and more flexible. Still, there are a scant few things that I am not ready to release into the great cosmic dustbin. So, thank you, elf or fairy or sprite or whomever it was who put my favorite necklace back in my path this morning. I'm a believer in everyday magic.

WRINKLE, WRINKLE, LITTLE SCAR

Wrinkle, wrinkle, little scar,
How I wonder why you are.
Up above my furrowed brow,
Framed around my smiling mouth.
So many tales you have to tell,
Of love, and loss, and life lived well.
Wrinkle, Wrinkle, Little Scar,
How I wonder that you are.

THE UNBEARABLE LIGHTNESS OF LETTING GO

As time passes, I find my focus shifting away from the physical and toward the ephemeral. I find myself less worried about my wrinkles and more concerned with my legacy. What footprint will I leave behind, if any? Either way, does it matter?

If I do leave a footprint, I sure as hell hope it's deeper than Instagram selfies or Pinterest-friendly DIY ideas.

Perhaps this is what happens as our "beauty fades," because it does, regardless of futile attempts to prevent it from fading. Unless you're Christie Brinkley, in which case, I'll have whatever the hell she's having— Or not, because there is something powerful about losing the desire to please other people. It's kind of delightful not having to be pretty anymore. It's freeing. It's transformative.

It's also a huge money saver. Magical skin creams are fucking expensive.

I am also less interested in owning stuff. Don't get me wrong: I still like stuff, but I'm less inclined to drag it home and put it on a shelf. I can appreciate it without needing to possess it. Even though I keep de-stashing, there is still so much stuff left. I worry about other people having to deal with the stuff I might leave behind. I want to be lighter, freer, less weighed down. I don't want my legacy to be a hoard of glitter tubes or a bin full of shoes.

I find petty grievances and small slights less worthy of my attention. I'm less inclined to care if people agree with me. My worldview is not defined by how many likes or shares it generates. My positions are more flexible and less dependent on their alignment with the status quo. I am less inclined to demand that others share my worldview, and more inclined to agree to disagree.

Neither preaching to the choir nor arguing with fools are worthy endeavors. Better to join the choir in a joyful noise and leave the fools to argue among themselves.

As time passes, I find that my sense of self-importance diminishes. I realize that my life is just a tiny, almost imperceptible blip on the grand cosmic radar, and I'm learning to embrace that. I take myself less seriously. The need to be right fades in importance. I appreciate the tragi-comical absurdity of day-to-day life.

The more I let go, the more space I make for love to move in and expand. I am lighter and lighter. My ego shrinks as my heart grows. The word *I* becomes less powerful than the word *we*. The importance of civic duty increases. The stewardship of the planet means more than the stewardship of stuff. The fight to protect kindness, joy, truth, freedom, and equality becomes far more urgent than the desire to protect myself.

The unbearable lightness of letting go becomes more bearable with each release. As I inch toward the finish line, I hope to arrive free of attachment and filled with so much love that I expand into the great cosmic is-ness and lose my "self" in it forever.

I did hedge my bets by writing this book, which may or may not make it past the first printing. Ah, the irony is rich.

ACKNOWLEDGMENTS

Thank you to my stalwart editor Jennifer Williams for encouraging me to pursue this book and holding my hand through the arduous process of editing my epic manuscript and finding a title we could all embrace.

ABOUT THE AUTHOR

Three notches too loud, five notches too sparkly, aging disgracefully, Margot Potter is either a Renaissance woman or a jill-of-all-trades. It depends on which day you ask her. When she's not arranging words into sentences, she's been known to make crafty magic, trip the boards, ham it up for the camera, and croon a happy tune. She has a shameless love of glitter and neon pom-poms. Her hobbies include rescuing dogs, collecting shoes, whipping up tasty cocktails, stalking oceanfront properties online, and thrift-store shopping. Margot has written seven books on jewelry making and design and an e-book on personal branding. She's appeared on local and national TV as a design expert, and she spent 11 years as an on-air product expert at QVC.